FROM MILTON KEYNES TO MANHATTAN

CONRAN&PARTNERS

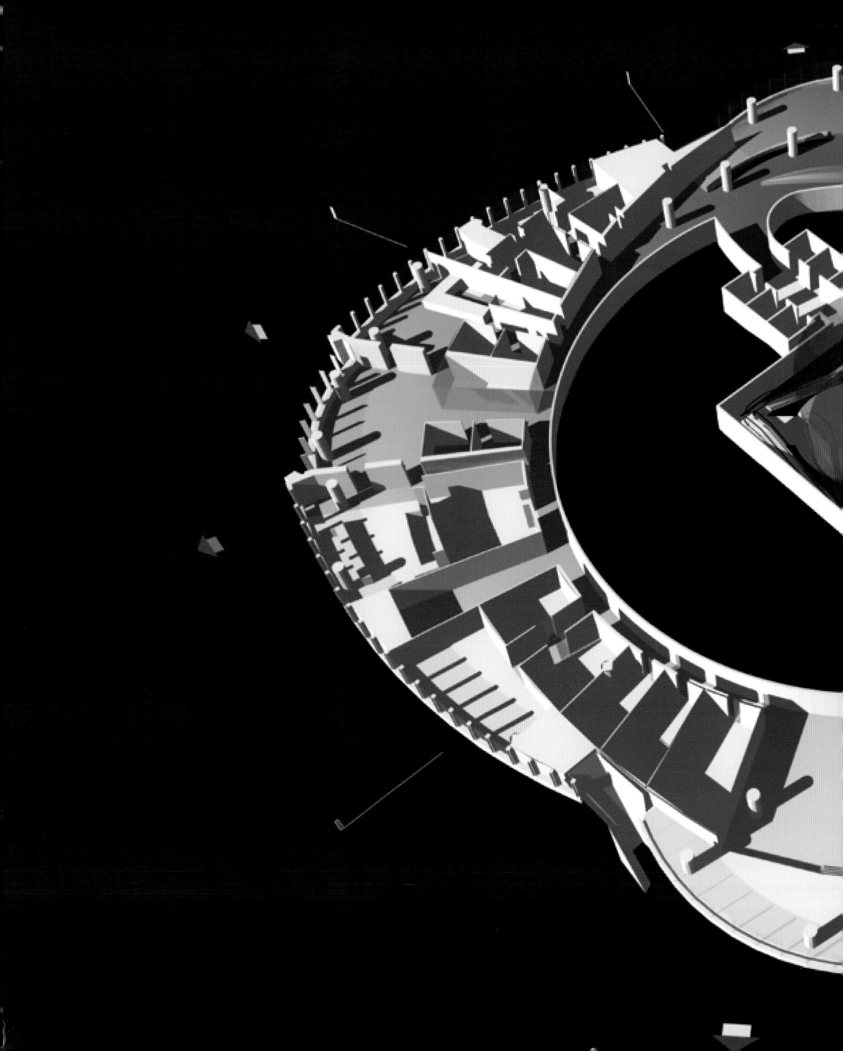

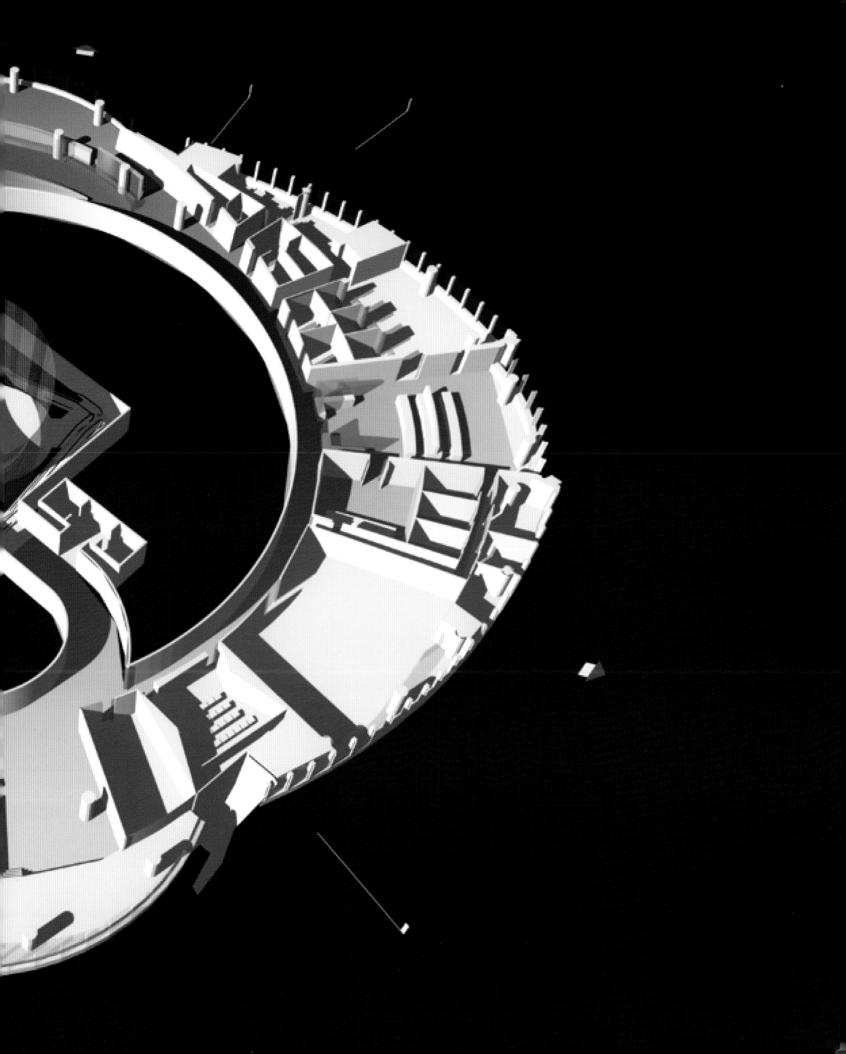

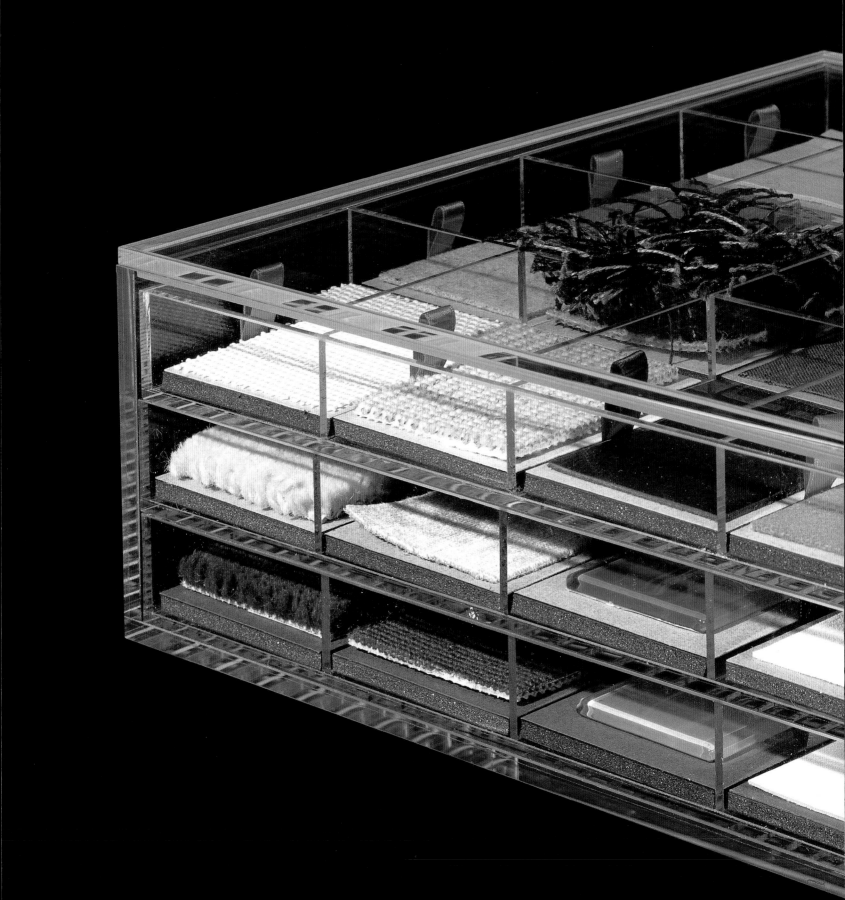

Previous pages   Roppongi Club
51st floor
Mori Tower, Tokyo

Roppongi Club
Material samples

Roppongi Club
Material samples

Roppongi Club
View of office pods

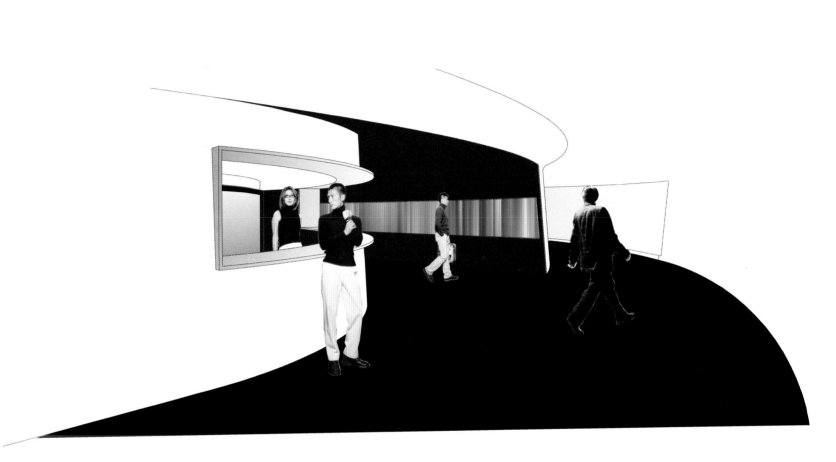

NO HOUSE STYLE BUT A HISTORY. NOT A FIXED POSITION, BUT A FOCUS ON QUESTIONING WHAT GOES ON WHEN ONE TAKES A JOURNEY FROM PAST TO PRESENT. WHAT PROCESS OF CHANGE OCCURS? WHY MIGHT ONE WANT TO CHANGE? THIS BOOK AIMS TO EXPLORE THE WORK OF A GLOBAL, MULTI-DISCIPLINARY ARCHITECTURAL PRACTICE. EVOLVED OVER 21 YEARS, CONRAN & PARTNERS' ARCHITECTURE, URBAN AND INTERIOR DESIGN ADHERES TO A COMMITMENT TO WHAT ARCHITECTURAL CRITIC DEYAN SUDJIC CALLS "MAKING PLACES THAT ARE ALIVE".

Introduction

The architectural trajectory of Conran & Partners encompassed two phases of existence, from the early days of Conran Roche, to its expansion as CD Partnership, before being renamed and developing further under its current identity. During this time the type and range of work undertaken by the practice has expanded hugely in brief, location and approach. Concentrating on the architectural activities of the practice since its inception in 1980, this book has developed with a recognition that product and graphic design are key to its work. The title, *From Milton Keynes to Manhattan*, is intended to evoke the spirit of that path. Point A represents an award winning new town in the UK, highly significant in architectural terms, and one where the practice began its work under the name of Conran Roche. Point B is in New York, an urbane location on another continent, and a setting where, as Conran & Partners, the practice recently worked on a disused piece of city under the Queensboro Bridge, creating a new architecture as part of the Bridgemarket complex. Both these urban locations – one wholly new, the other redundant but made into a lively piece of urbanism – have relevance to the history of architecture in their adherence to pioneering and distinctive schemes.

Both locations embody ideas about how a city can be a place to live and work in. The hypothetical trip that the title describes represents not only a jump in type and scale of urban project, but also a mental leap in developing a philosophy about the relationship between architectural design and the city, between theory and practice in a given context and between the past and present.

The modernist approach to architecture employed by Conran Roche, with its emphasis on classicism and axiality, has been enhanced in the work of Conran & Partners by an approach that focuses on the context of each individual project. Architecture in general is now much more about questioning – about how different functions relate to each other? – and about adopting a basic curiosity concerning fundamental activities, such as work and leisure. One of the results of this approach is the a need for a new architectural vocabulary. In attempting a fresh perspective on multi-disciplinary design, long after the end of the Modernist Project, and at a time of increased focus on urban regeneration and the quality of urban life, it is insightful to look at Conran & Partners' body of work as indicative of a more understated, individual and flexible approach to architecture.

If architecture is still able to play a role in improving people's lives, as Conran & Partners are convinced it is, then that somewhat ambiguous but essential phrase "urban regeneration" deserves closer attention. It is clear, particularly from looking at some of Conran & Partners' urban projects, such as Butlers Wharf, that the practice utilises the past, present and future through what can be referred to as a process of 'architectural proliferation'. That is, taking the existing fabric and current conditions and rather than replacing them, creating a synthesis of elements so as to evolve a new urban condition – i.e. how do you *grow* a piece of city, rather than how you *build* it?

This situation requires a new language, as well as a new way of navigating and thinking about the urban scene as a whole. Conran & Partners aim to apply solutions on an individual basis, but also employ a variety of skills in tandem with architecture, such as urban planning, interior design, graphic design, brand design, exhibition design and scenography. This development has been facilitated by the substantial and pro-active product and graphic design arm of the company. At the same time, the practice's experience in designing a complete range of leisure environments has evolved, with their approach to planning remaining pragmatic and sensible – they provide a rigorous architecture where the interior surfaces matter acutely. This is part of a philosophy that says "spend money where it counts" focusing on the surfaces people touch and see at close range.

The practice's buildings tend not to shout, rather they are more likely to play a role in the mending and restoration of the urban fabric. In order to make that mending adaptive in the future, these buildings need to have a sound infrastructure. The modernist leanings of Conran Roche helped the practice realise schemes that are clearly and sensibly planned. However, a full-blown modern movement approach to on architecture means consistency through and through, and a continuity in the use of language. By contrast, Conran & Partners quite deliberately take a different position. This involves a strong interest in the experience of space, in particular, how to create spatial compositions engaging human interest, exuding both legibility and warmth in public and private environments. These often employ narratives how the different spaces of a building can be experienced. This method places a value in allowing an element of spontaneity in the process of making architecture, finding things of interest as projects develop, and allowing them to feed back into the design.

One of the main aspects of Conran & Partners' work has been their restaurants and food outlets. Making a satisfying place in which to eat, drink, socialise and affirm one's place in a changing cultural *milieu* is a strong theme within the practice's body of work over the last six years. A restaurant is a stage set in many respects, yet one that has to be convincing as a public space. The restaurants and bars designed by Conran & Partners have largely been for their chairman Terence Conran's restaurant company, a uniquely supportive situation, in which he has been both initiator and patron. Conran's own approach to design is highly intuitive. However, the interpretative skill the practice applies to briefs for restaurant projects in a variety of international locations requires much more than a flair for scenography and the processional quality of space universally desired by such environments.

Achieving local credibility is a tall order, and to survive a design must go deeply into every detail, and propose something thoroughly robust and yet magical. At the same time the brief for each of the restaurants has been based on a clearly defined business plan. Clients' growing abilities to focus their own aspirations through design, not just in this area, but every area of lifestyle design, has meant that architecture has become, increasingly, about responding to needs on all levels. Aesthetics cannot be divorced from function.

How does a designer effectively import a stylistic rationale and make it as credible within a local cultural context as the food being served or displayed? To make such an interior work in this way, Conran & Partners define and develop what they call a "thematic". At the Great Eastern Hotel, for instance, the sheer number of restaurants and bars called for multiple branding. Always, however, there is a rational spatial framework and a choice of materials and detailing that is sensuous and fits the thematic. This can be contrasted with the slick, standardised and hyper-real 'themed' environment, such as the futuristic spaceship of London's Trocadero, where the 'logic' of brand development is taken to the limit – both at the level of product and as a concept that aims to be spatialised. In promoting the value of the architect making an individual creative response, Conran & Partners also avoid the pitfalls of "glocal design". For, when multinationals and their brands take over large areas of the centres of cities, what often results is a growing sameness within the built environment.

Just looking at London's skyline from atop the London Eye, the viewer is struck by how few buildings really transcend the normative condition to express a full-blown extravagance. This is not to say that every urban building has to aggressively advertise itself, for as Eldred Evans once said, "very few buildings need to be important in the urban fabric; a hierarchy of kinds is desirable". If, though, a public building needs to advertise its presence, the bold, slightly radical appearance of the Metropolitan in Glasgow provides a good example. Big boxes on stilts clad in metals, stone and render, attached to a car park with a complex random range of punctured materials, brighten up a dark backland area of the city. The boxes as an architectural rationale and an interpretation of a modernist agenda is the starting point of the building, but it is the diversification within the design that creates its unique urban character.

Night view
Metropolitan scheme,
Glasgow

Street view
Kamiyamacho apartment
Tokyo

Corner view
Kamiyamacho apartment
Tokyo

Conran & Partners would also distance themselves from current tactics whereby 'innovative' form and a connection to site give way to the precedence of symmetry and discipline. For, sometimes, say, in a city like Tokyo, there is no context or grid to refer to and so Conran & Partners used natural colours from the surrounding landscape as a focus for the design of their Kamiyamacho apartment building. As a result, the decision to use the soft contrasting tones of stone, copper and timber – three claddings used as distinct elements within the apartment building – lends a surprising richness to an otherwise unremarkable low-rise area of the city. The design is not inventing a sculptural aesthetic as in the work of Frank Gehry; it is more polite, but at the same time expressive. Architects are not generally trained in colour theory, but as a skill it represents a major design tool. A scheme of this kind – with subtle, earthy colours, not just any chromatic solution, but those already existing in the Japanese environment – brings vivid references from nature to the grey mass of Tokyo's architecture.

It is clear that as far as Conran & Partners are concerned buildings, particularly in towns and cities are, and will remain, essentially the result of a bespoke activity, each one individually governed by its site, orientation and brief, or combination of uses. Design skills can and must be used to create differentiated, freely interactive and individualistic spaces. Purity and rigour, narrative and the sensuous – these concerns co-exist in the work of the practice. In their interiors, materials may be mass produced, but they are also crafted. They impress that considerable care has gone into the assemblage of a space – contributing to a more sophisticated and yet accessible architectural language. This is a key to many of Conran & Partners' projects. A fundamental part of this is detailing, whether floor tiles, or cladding. Whatever form it takes, it is always chosen so as to relate to context. Architecture can get carried away with self-reference, but in the body of work shown here, no attempts are made to fetishise technology or the signs of construction for their own sake.

It is the aim of this book, then, to investigate and illuminate the full range of Conran & Partners' approach to architecture, interior and urban design in their conception, planning, composition and execution of a wide range of projects. As such, *From Milton Keynes to Manhattan*, is testimony to Conran & Partners' success in combining a committed set of architectural concerns with a marked appreciation of, and adapbility to, a variety of contexts.

HISTORY

Conran & Partners as a practice originated as Conran Roche, an architectural and town planning firm established by Fred Roche and Terence Conran in 1980. The influence of former Director of Architecture Stuart Mosscrop, in particular – with his rationalist roots and views on architecture's larger cultural role – cannot be overstated. Roche was more the strategic businessman, whilst Mosscrop, an 'architect's architect', took command of the building process. It was Mosscrop's strong views about how Butlers Wharf should be developed, for instance, that informed the sympathetic quality of its transformation.

Of the body of significant buildings the practice has produced over the last 21 years, many of the early ones were in Milton Keynes, where Mosscrop and Roche had been working for the Development Corporation, designing buildings for the new city centre. Richard Doone, now Managing Director, Paul Zara and Matthew Wood, both Directors, joined in the mid-to late 1980s. Former Director James Soane and Associate Director Sarah Aldridge joined in the early 1990s. They were involved in several of the buildings that helped the practice develop a considerable reputation. Landmark Place, a pair of speculative offices constructed around the new city church in Milton Keynes, and the result of a competition win, is one such project. Earlier buildings included the headquarters for the Institute of Chartered Accountants, 1984, and the County Court and Post House Hotel, 1986.

At this time the practice's work was wholly located in the UK, a period well before their international projects, such as Das Triest Hotel, Vienna or Bridgemarket, New York. A body of Japanese work for the Mori Building Company, one of the most active property developers in Tokyo, emerged in the late 1990s. The ratio of work obtained through the Conran companies has now reduced to 20% from its peak of 75% in the early 1990s. However, the Conran companies were the chief early clients for the practice, commissioning them to refurbish an historic building in Cambridge's city centre for Habitat, and a distribution centre for Mothercare.

The many urban refurbishment projects tackled by the practice further fuelled their interest in issues of context and the play between the old and new. It is these concerns that rapidly became major threads in their work, defining an entire approach to architecture and urban context in subsequent years. In the mid-1980s the practice converted the former tyre depot at Brompton Cross on the Fulham Road into the now famous Michelin House, home to the Conran Shop's flagship outlet, the Bibendum restaurant and, on new upper floors, Hamlyn Publishing's offices. English Heritage supported the conversion, approving the Conran Roche scheme (put together with YRM Partnership, joint architect on the project). The proposal included a simple and under-stated treatment of the new façade, using mullionless glass, and full length windows on the inner surface, providing a view of the original listed wall, while at the same time avoiding a pastiche of the original vigorous elevations. Brompton Cross, with the arrival soon after of Joseph and Issey Miyake, became a space with many open glazed frontages, a proud symbol of the new love affair between fashion retail and design.

Much of the practice's work during the 1980s was devoted to the regeneration of Butlers Wharf. This scheme – on an 11 acre site with nineteenth century warehouses on the south bank of the Thames close to Tower Bridge – received the most media acclaim during this period. In the context of the texture of London's inner city, the project, which is within the Tower Bridge conservation area, is a good precursor of the high density, 'brownfield' schemes now promoted by government and planning policy. Notably, earlier redevelopment proposals for the site had failed due to their requirement for demolition of most of the area, an approach the practice would not entertain.

In developing their masterplan, the practice proposed keeping the 11 listed buildings in the area and creating new buildings alongside that would draw new life and activity to this part of Central London's southern riverbank. What was developed is a clear demonstration of the practice's ability to create high quality, high density urban infrastructure – a successful integration into the existing street pattern of new buildings and sensitively converted grade II listed nineteenth century warehouses. The practice converted the Butler's Wharf building next to the Thames into flats and offices, with a highly popular river frontage of restaurants. These backed onto an upgraded street soon to be filled itself with a proliferation of restaurants, bars, art galleries, and, behind these, housing blocks and landscaped public spaces. The area is now almost seen as a heritage zone, as though it had always existed in this gentrified form.

At the end of Shad Thames to the east, the Design Museum, the world's first museum focusing on design, was set up in what had been a disused 1950s warehouse. This stark white structure, still prominent from across Tower Bridge, is notable in that it emerged from a period in the early 1980s when the variegated language of postmodernism was still rife. The conversion was not tongue-in-cheek, however, with the use of render, glass blocks and marble genuinely paying homage to the Bauhaus legacy. Two floors of galleries, a café and shop with the Blueprint Café on the first floor, it felt clean, rational and deceptively like a new building. Here was stated a stylistic adherence to a rational architectural approach – the provision of a simple plan without noise. Phil Tabor, who wrote one of the most comprehensive critiques of the project at the time of its opening, referred to its "gleaming, rather nautical mass", and commented that the "detailing throughout is so understated that at times it only just avoids meanness". However, he applauded overall "the reticent strength of the architects' language" and the building's "spirit of quiet ordinariness and light". The Design Museum provided a space that could be transformed, and now, nearly 12 years later, there are ongoing projects involving the practice in maximising the site's potential.

The Blueprint Café was refurbished in 1997 to create more table room on the terrace and enlarge the kitchen. To achieve this in a tight space, the architects created a glass 'gallery', an all-weather extension that responds to the direct and unembellished language of the museum. The challenge was to provide this extra facility without compromising the quality of the original work. The added enclosure is made of a white steel frame with a glass roof and sliding glass doors: in summer these can be opened, letting air circulate; in winter, yellow blinds can be drawn across the roof. It is a simply executed enlargement, and there is no desire to manipulate form into a visual conceit. A large mirror at the end of the space reflects the spectacular aspect of Tower Bridge.

The downturn in the property market at the start of the 1990s meant that the full scope of the project, in particular the spectacular Spice Quay office building, intended to be the focal point of the development, did not progress. The practice continued their role as masterplanners, producing a proposal that was predominantly residential in nature and represented an attempt to regenerate interest in the area. With the regaining in strength of the residential market, the remaining sites have now since been developed as housing, and some of the earlier mixed use schemes proposed did not come to fruition. However, along with the successful injection of residential schemes and restaurants into an area previously totally bereft of such facilities, the masterplan brought shops, new offices and workshops, two museums, student accommodation for the London School of Economics and a community nursery.

The character and siting of buildings such as Saffron Wharf, a new five storey office building designed for flexible use on the western side of St Saviour's Dock, reflects the practice's concern for architectural regeneration as a mode of rebalancing the urban fabric. Saffron Wharf takes the form of a cube planted into the more disorganised structure of the street. As with their urban refurbishment projects generally, the process of looking back is not with the intention of reproducing old form, but to synthesise that found with something new. Architecture critic Catherine Slessor, who wrote about Butlers Wharf in 1990, would concur with this. She saw the projects as being concerned to "introduce a catholic spread of uses in the guise of both new and existing structures, while attempting to preserve the original fragile geometry of the streets". The driving motive behind the progressive programme of Butlers Wharf was to achieve a good balance between building form, density as a urban pattern and use. The mixed element of the scheme proved harder to realise. However, what is vital for such a major urban experiment is that, as Slessor underlines, "the potential exists to create something which might just turn out to be as messy, urban and vital as a piece of real city".

Night view
Michelin House
London

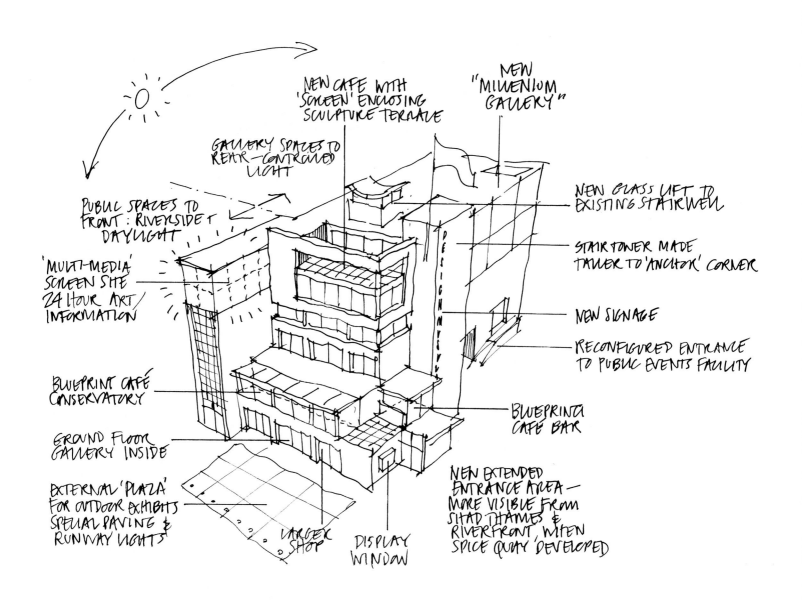

NEW CAFE WITH 'SCREEN' ENCLOSING SCULPTURE TERRACE

NEW "MILLENIUM GALLERY"

GALLERY SPACES TO REAR - CONTROLED LIGHT

PUBLIC SPACES TO FRONT : RIVERSIDE + DAYLIGHT

NEW GLASS LIFT TO EXISTING STAIRWELL

STAIR TOWER MADE TALLER TO 'ANCHOR' CORNER

'MULTI-MEDIA' SCREEN SITE 24 HOUR ART/ INFORMATION

NEW SIGNAGE

RECONFIGURED ENTRANCE TO PUBLIC EVENTS FACILITY

BLUEPRINT CAFE CONSERVATORY

BLUEPRINT CAFE BAR

GROUND FLOOR GALLERY INSIDE

NEW EXTENDED ENTRANCE AREA — MORE VISIBLE FROM SHAD THAMES & RIVERFRONT, WHEN SPICE QUAY 'DEVELOPED'

EXTERNAL 'PLAZA' FOR OUTDOOR EXHIBITS SPECIAL PAVING & RUNWAY LIGHTS

LARGER SHOP

DISPLAY WINDOW

Competition sketch
Design Museum

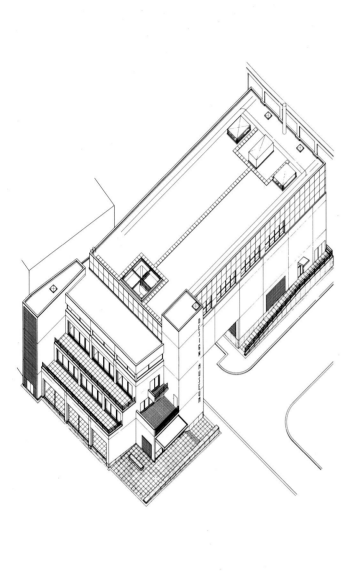

AXONOMETRIC

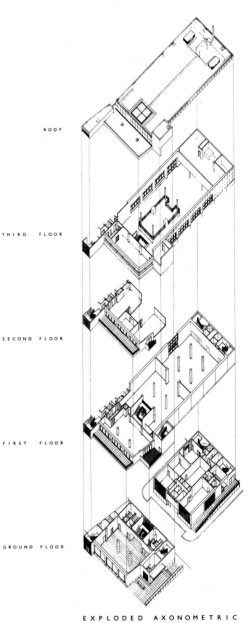

ROOF

THIRD FLOOR

SECOND FLOOR

FIRST FLOOR

GROUND FLOOR

EXPLODED AXONOMETRIC

Axonometric
Design Museum

Original plans

Existing warehouse
before re-furbishment

Design Museum
with new Blueprint Café
extension, 2001

Coriander Building

Saffron Wharf
St Saviour's Dock

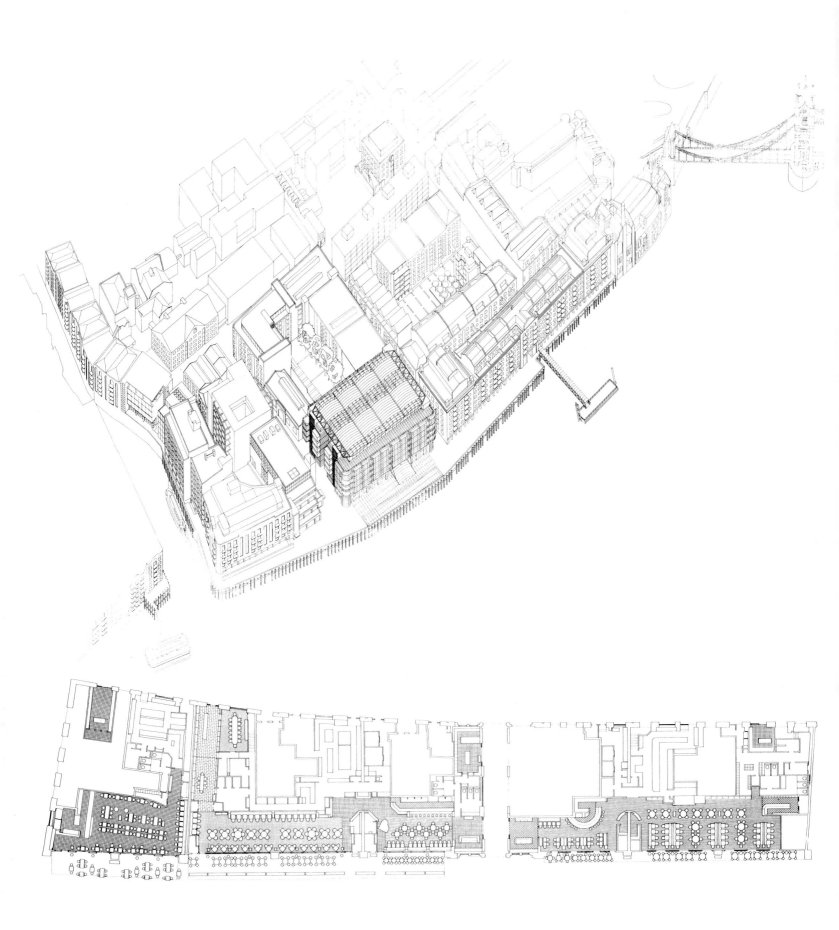

Isometric view
Butlers Wharf
Master plan

Ground floor plan
Butlers Wharf Building
Restaurant layouts

Butlers Wharf
View

Longman headquarters

The Longman headquarters forms a threshold between the town of Harlow and a wide stretch of meadow behind. At the forefront of 'green' office concepts at the time it was completed, the building, with its 16,000 square metres of office space, located around three atria, represented one of the UK's most environmentally friendly work places. The reason behind the building was the relocation of 900 staff from offices in and around London to one location in central Harlow. Working with the client to change the culture of the organisation from an environment of diversity, consisting of mainly small cellular spaces, the architects introduced large, open plan floor plates. Naturally ventilated, the building's expressed, reinforced concrete structure assists in cooling by utilising its thermal mass. Relatively high floor-to-ceiling heights in each office allow warm air to rise above the general working area. It is then drawn into the atria, which allows it to flow up and out of roof vents, at the same time bringing fresh air into the offices.

Ideas about how to treat an elevation were garnered from the Milton Keynes days and fed into the project. Longman remains to this day a handsome building, finished in Cornish granite and Jura limestone, with a metal clad fifth floor. One cannot help inspecting the interior at length – in particular the windows – for further signs of the building's much vaunted green status. Aluminium-framed, the windows are double glazed, with each bay incorporating high and low level opening lights to give local control. External louvre shades reduce the heat gain from high-angle summer sun, while allowing low-angle winter sun to enter the building and assist with its heating. The ecology of the office building is its major theme, treated both as an environmental and social quality. This was a low-energy approach to architectural design with which the Powergen headquarters in Coventry, built at around the same time as Longman (by architect Rab Bennetts) shares some similarities. Both are out of London, on greenfield sites, and both use their structure for visual and servicing purposes. Other architectural practices including Feilden Clegg, DEGW and Jestico+Whiles also made 'green', energy efficient buildings a primary focus of their work during this period.

Longman
Concept sketches

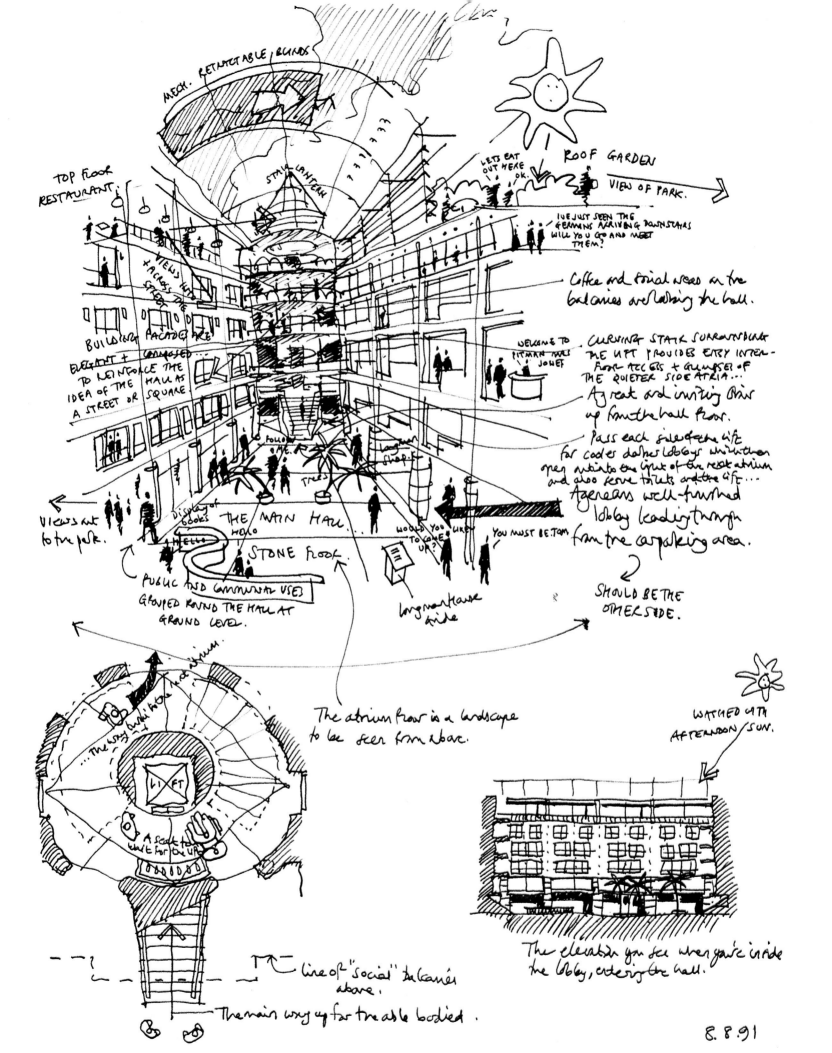

MECH. RETRACTABLE BLINDS

TOP FLOOR RESTAURANT.

STAIR LANTERN

ROOF GARDEN

LETS EAT OUT HERE OK.

VIEW OF PARK.

IVE JUST SEEN THE GERMANS ARRIVING DOWNSTAIRS WILL YOU GO AND MEET THEM?

VIEWS ACROSS THE STREET

BUILDING FACADES ARE ELEGANT + COMPOSED ... TO REINFORCE THE IDEA OF THE HALL AS A STREET OR SQUARE

WELCOME TO PITMAN MRS JONES

Coffee and tovial used on the balconies overlooking the hall.

CURVING STAIR SURROUNDING THE LIFT PROVIDES EASY INTER-FLOOR ACCESS + GLIMPSES OF THE QUIETER SIDE ATRIA...

A great and inviting stair up from the hall floor.

Pass each side of the lift for cooler darker lobbies which then open out into the light of the next atrium and also serve toilets and the lift...

A generous well-finished lobby leading through from the carparking area.

FOLLOW ME. R.

Display of books

THE MAIN HALL ...

Longman shop.

TREES

HELLO

HELLO

STONE FLOOR.

WOULD YOU LIKE TO COME UP?

YOU MUST BE TOM

VIEWS OUT to the park.

PUBLIC AND COMMUNAL USES GROUPED ROUND THE HALL AT GROUND LEVEL.

Longman House side

SHOULD BE THE OTHER SIDE.

the way turn into the atrium

LIFT

A seat to wait for the lift

The atrium floor is a landscape to be seen from above.

WATCHED WITH AFTERNOON SUN.

Line of "social" balconies above.

The main way up for the able bodied.

The elevation you see when you're inside the lobby, entering the hall.

8.8.91

THF Hotel,
Milton Keynes

following pages
in order

County Court Building,
Milton Keynes

ICA building,
Milton Keynes

Longman Building
Exterior and atrium

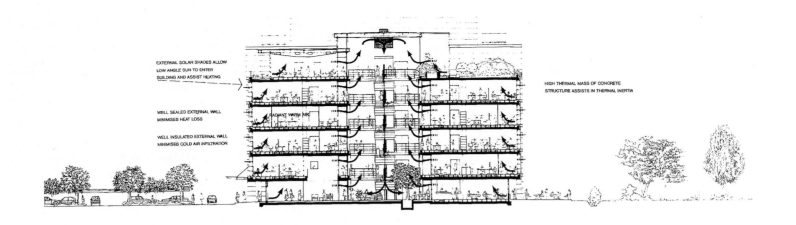

EXTERNAL SOLAR SHADES ALLOW
LOW ANGLE SUN TO ENTER
BUILDING AND ASSIST HEATING

HIGH THERMAL MASS OF CONCRETE
STRUCTURE ASSISTS IN THERMAL INERTIA

WELL SEALED EXTERNAL WALL
MINIMISES HEAT LOSS

RADIANT WARM AIR

WELL INSULATED EXTERNAL WALL
MINIMISES COLD AIR INFILTRATION

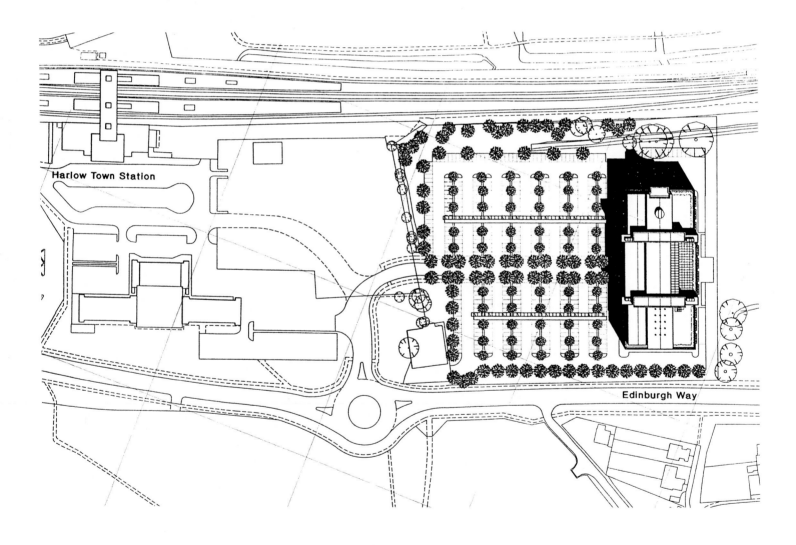

Harlow Town Station

Edinburgh Way

Longman Building
Cross section and site plan

42

Multi-displinary Marriage

The merger of Conran Roche with a team of interior and graphic designers in 1993 created CD Partnership at Shad Thames. This phase of the practice's development was also characterised by the more active role of Terence Conran. The downturn in new building work brought on by the recession precipitated an expansion of interior projects and allowed the practice to explore how the logical and the intuitive could work together in the generation of architectural schemes, injecting a sensuality into the rational design approach inherited from Conran Roche.

This major transition, played out in the context of a new marriage of disciplines, meant that fault lines between all the constituent professions could be usefully tested. Product design skills, with their focus on the compatibility of elements working together, were and are badly needed in interior design projects; graphic design's emphasis on 'language' and legibility can help give a particular gearing to the social communication of a project – each enhances the other. This mix of skills led to passionate discussions about design within the project teams at CD Partnership, with the desire for architectural rigour struggling alongside an eclectic approach to design.

The heritage of the practice's early body of work possesses an extraordinary homogeneity and purity. Finely constructed, earlier projects lean towards the generic or the abstract, in line with the older, clearly defined boundary of the architectural profession. The coherence of the body of Milton Keynes buildings, well proportioned, and using good quality, natural materials, shows a keen understanding of the aspirations of this new city. However, Conran & Partners has since transcended the necessity to be quite so homogeneous in this way. They have found a freedom to explore and organise all sorts of overlaps and convergences in their interests. Their ability to apply a diversity of skills to projects in the public realm means the inherited tactics informing the humanely designed working environment of Milton Keynes have been reappraised in the light of social developments, both within the practice and a wider architectural context.

The Longman building was the end point of a process, as well as an open door into a new era. What makes the project significant in the practice's lineage is its role as a test-bed for some of the new ideas about architecture and interior design that can be seen in the their work throughout the 1990s, such as the Conran Shop at Marylebone. Longman's structural ideas were filtered through from one to the other, and, indeed, on to subsequent projects.

However, the recession in the early 1990s almost completely halted the supply of these large architectural projects, and like many of their contemporaries, Conran & Partners experience a dramatic downturn in workload. During the ensuing lull, magazines like *Designers' Journal* and *Blueprint* focused their attentions on a flourishing interior design scene, driven initially by retail as the recession eased. Opportunities to engage the public realm through large-scale design were limited in the UK.

As the 1990s progressed, urban fabric and identity never seemed so manipulable. Locations in the city were reinvented. The media became a crucible of 'lifestyle' culture, fuelled first by the specialist and then picked up on by the national media. Inventing the city as a place of endless cultural, social and spatial possibilities required a constant wave of new shops, bars, restaurants, clubs and housing. The work of developers like the Manhattan Loft Company in London and Urban Splash in Manchester gave physical form to social patterns already crystalling, such as the trend towards increasing numbers of people living alone, and triggered more far-reaching economic regeneration of depressed industrial areas. With this came the need for social facilities providing for niche markets in each 'revised' location.

It may be more commonplace now for younger architectural practices to straddle a wide range of commercial fields experiencing buoyancy and a receptiveness to new lifestyle concepts. In that sense architecture in the UK has seen its role in marketing spaces through the use of design skills come of age. Credibility in the profession has, traditionally, most easily come by specialising in one field. As one of the most generalist professions, architecture needs to move beyond this convention, and become as multi-disciplinary as possible, pooling skills in order to provide an inclusive approach to context at all scales. Along with an increasing number of projects closely wedded to 'lifestyle', the practice is also committed to hybrid projects that bring new design into the traditional fabric of the city, such as housing. This is equally applicable to major new building projects such as Ocean Terminal which address the wider urban environment. The common feature here is that architecture is providing new contexts in such a way as to enable cities to straddle social change.

By offering competence in all these areas, there is the risk that a practice's identity could become unclear. However, to be versatile and operate effectively on a number of levels is also a seductive proposition. A series of projects gave the practice increasing opportunities to work on architectural interventions in historic structures, converting them into shops, restaurants and bars. The gastrodome, restaurant, bar and private club created out of the semi-derelict Bluebird Garage, on the Kings Road, Europe's biggest motor garage of the 1920s, is a good example. Michelin House is a London landmark, and Bluebird now also shares that status, in its impact on the surrounding area in terms of quality of built environment as well as retail values. Here, within the shell of an historic building, the practice was able to explore ideas of circulation, and the combination of prosaic and sensuous materials so as to add life to the existing architecture. The courtyard in the front of the garage – which Matthew Wood refers to as "a small piece of city" – demanded a sound landscape solution. The form of a market stall provided this – nothing like an urban 'green' space, but a space, given the context, for new public use.

Wolverton Gardens
Office building
Hammersmith

The Conran Shop, on Marylebone High Street, is an entirely new building constructed behind a retained façade of red brick and terracotta tile, and a scheme which also houses Conran's Orrery restaurant on its first floor. Here, the ideas of construction explored by Doone in Longman were developed to a high degree of sophistication, achieving a subtle beauty in the use of exposed pre-cast concrete. The project displays an astute way of retaining a façade, while behind it dropping a spatially well defined building that does not cramp its context. The combined use of unpainted, fair faced concrete and pre-cast concrete planks at each structural bay, built up in components, relates to the design of Longman, where concrete soffits are exposed, and floor voids are used for the primary services. The language of a raised floor with its pre-cast slabs underneath and in-situ beams and columns is radical for a retail space. Not only was a level concrete soffit with minimal depth achieved, but there is a little difference between the appearance of the in-situ work and pre-cast concrete. It was decided to leave the structure exposed as an architectural feature, including the fair-faced vaulted ceiling which also allowed for greater headroom. Like Longman, the shop is a building where large areas of glazing and the concrete soffit maximise natural light, making for a comfortable interior that is nonetheless underlined by an industrial aesthetic.

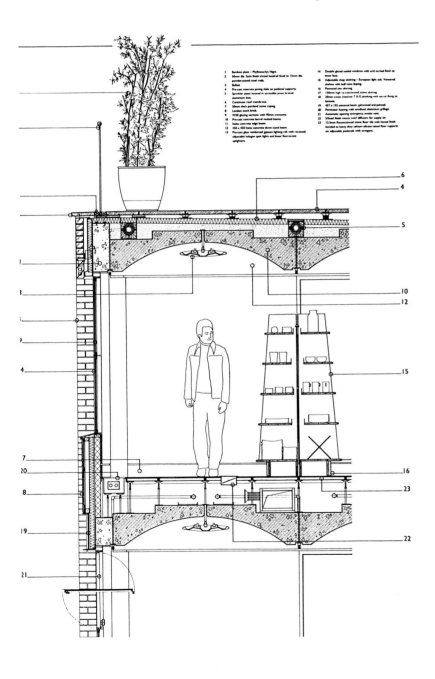

Detailed cross section
of typical concrete bay

The second floor is set back from both the High Street and the mews at the rear of the building, so as to reduce its impact on the surrounding area. Part glazed and part clad in aluminium panels to further emphasise its lightness, this floor is provided with doors that, in the summer, can be opened to look down over the restaurant, which in turn can extend its operation out onto the second floor terrace. Orrery, provides a particular example of a legible collaged environment. Screens with aerofoil tilting panels – inspired by Eileen Gray, a curved, repeating roof, collections of papier-maché bottles – a la Morandi – all provide the diner with visual interests. Velvet upholstery and coloured leather bolsters add further playful comfort. On the face of it, the restaurant's space is comprised of dense detail, but in practice it works as an organised set of references that work as a whole.

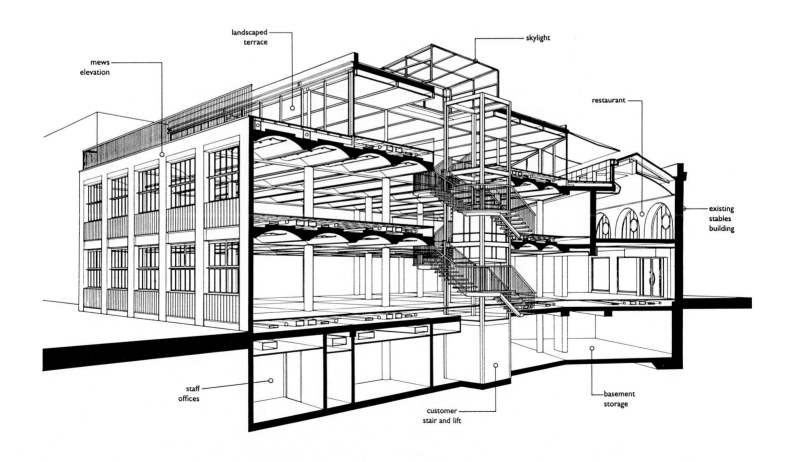

Cut away perspective
The Conran Shop
Marylebone

Construction shots
The Conran Shop
Marylebone

Elevation
Marylebone High Street

Internal vertical
circulation

Integrated Interiors

The repertoire of structural and material elements in a design is something that must be balanced, however necessary a palette of detail is to generate atmosphere, particularly in the micro-scale of a restaurant or hotel. Four restaurants – Sartoria, Coq d'Argent, Lenbach and Alcazar – all in central city locations, embody this desire. Sartoria, completed in 1998, took over the old Knoll showroom on the corner of Savile Row and New Burlington Street. Its inspiration came from Italian Rationalism, with the space full of crisp clean lines and square detailing. Here, bowing to the tradition of Savile Row, the architects play with the idea of tailoring. A measuring tape motif makes its way onto ashtrays, a pin design onto the menus, and button motifs are etched on the glasses. The visitor is greeted by a glass screen reminiscent of a tailors' dummy before swiftly discovering two quite stout real ones, one male and one female – perhaps a cautionary note, posed behind.

This kind of trickery is kept well in balance by the overall design and the gravitas of the materials, including pale open Biancone marble on the counters and travertine on the floor, dark stained oak panelling, and leather for the reception box. Carrying this palette through to the street, the restaurant's plate glass elevation is approached via a steel and etched glass ramp, with low level planting screening the diners behind bronze framed sliding windows. Sliding oak and glass screens for the private dining rooms, with wall panels covered in herringbone suiting material, add a further flourish to the environment.

In 1997, German clients approached the practice to turn part of the Lenbach Palace, a nineteenth century replica of an Italian palazzo in Munich, into a restaurant and nightclub. It is a project that can be understood in terms of the organisation of a complex narrative – the restaurant becomes a processional event, along the room's classical axis. Alcazar, a former printing house that became the well-known restaurant and cabaret bar of the same name during the 1970s, was the site of another conversion. Just off the Boulevard St Germain in Paris, its new role is a brasserie with the democratic feel Terence Conran favours.

Coq d'Argent, completed in 1998, is another London restaurant offering the aura associated with the most renowned New York restaurants. All the more so, for those in the know, given the controversial reputation of its setting, located on the roof of Stirling and Wilford's No 1 Poultry in the City of London, which was only built after notorious planning delays concerning Lord Palumbo's bid to give the City a contemporary architectural masterpiece. Coq d'Argent, primarily catering for City business customers, is reached via a lift opening on five landscaped terraces designed by Arabella Lennox-Boyd, which extend the restaurant into a verdant spacious public setting.

Sartoria restaurant
London

Interior view
Coq D'Argent

Roof top garden
Number 1 Poultry
City of London

Urban Consciousness

The idea that an urban consciousness can be embedded in microcosmic form in a design is played out in Das Triest Hotel, in Vienna. The refurbishment of a seventeenth century coaching house, Das Triest was the practice's first hotel outside the UK, and their first project abroad. Its significance lies in the scheme's regenerative qualities and style. A hotel is a place where fantasy and reality reside side by side, a place where design and detail are integral to the experience of the hotel as a whole. The client conceived of Das Triest as a retreat in the centre of the city, and asked the practice to design a new extension to the old 'house'. The result was perceived as a lot more radical in Vienna than it would have been in London – the Viennese refer to it as a "super-minimalist" project. The practice's attitude towards luxury and comfort was not overt, opulent or vulgar, a partial reaction to the Viennese tradition of the Baroque that has today degenerated into a faded kitsch. Rather the office, kitchen and service rooms front onto the street, with windows conceived of as display cases, suggesting the activities of the rooms behind. From the clear glass door to the bar one can see all the way through, across the lobby and into the restaurant – a direct and open attitude. By contrast, the hotel's front door is solid walnut, pierced by four square windows allowing only glimpses of the private world within.

Central Vienna

following pages   New glass entrance   Interior
Berns Restaurant   Berns Restaurant
Stockholm

A desire for new architecture to generate atmosphere underscores the practice's regeneration of the historic Bridgemarket, in the underbelly of Manhattan's Queensboro Bridge at 59th Street. The project is an open plan complex which includes Conran & Partners' designs for a new pavilion on the main plaza for The Conran Shop, and Guastavino's, a 600 seat collection of restaurants, bars and public rooms. Working with Hardy Holzman Pfeiffer Associates, the project architects who took charge of the restoration and adaptive re-use of the site, Conran & Partners' intervention revives a previously forgotten area of the city with an ambitious urban vision. Bridgemarket tries very hard to retain a sense of intimate scale in an environment designed to work well, both by day and night, and includes spaces for relaxation, meeting and other, incidental, activities. It brings together a piazza, a "pocket park" – designed to encourage congregation in a green urban setting – the shop, housed in a glass pavilion, which at night is evocatively lit to look like a museum display case, and a complex of eating and drinking facilities behind.

Bridgemarket is neither up-town nor down-town, to use Manhattan's local terminology for spatial character, but has its own distinction. On a similar scale and with a similar intention to Bluebird and the Michelin Building, Bridgemarket turns a redundant space in a location that previously lacked hybrid projects into a nodal point of gentrification that opens up the potential quality of the entire area. With notable exceptions, new and sophisticated destinations do not abound in New York City. Gentrification, in TriBeCa, for instance, can become sprawl. The cult of the individual building persists, to the detriment of street life. Land grabbing real estate and retail concerns occupy Manhattan, but rarely dovetail in such a way that an entire concept of attractive and welcoming public space is created in the process.

The Bridge, dating back to 1909, allows traffic to flow across the East River connecting mid-town with Queens. Underneath its arches, on the Manhattan side, are spaces comprising massive vaults faced in cream guastavino glazed terra-cotta tiles, from which the name of the restaurant was taken. Previously used as a market and then a storage depot – despite its having the scale and sculptural form of a cathedral – it was a virtually unknown pocket in the city. New architectural projects in New York involving the municipal authorities are frequently beset by bureaucratic delays. But because the space had been lying dormant for so long, the city's Landmarks Preservation Commission were keen to give Terence Conran and his restaurant group partner, Joel Kissin, the opportunity to build there. Designated a landmark in 1973, the bridge had been the subject of numerous proposals, all of which had fallen victim to the objections of local community boards. The 360 square metre new-build, single-storey glazed pavilion for The Conran Shop, and Bridgemarket's restaurants – with their vast arched windows – beneath the bridge, creates a dramatic juxtaposition of urban past and present. Through Conran & Partners' interventions, the nineteenth century engineering language of the bridge is connected with a lightweight, transparent architecture of the late twentieth century. The pavilion roof is a curved plane inset with glass block which lies in dynamic counterpoint to the climbing angle of the structure above. By night its apertures gently illuminate the bridge.

The space is cleanly designed, with timber and zinc fixtures and fittings. Guastavino's ensemble of restaurants and bars occupies 2,500 square metres of the dramatic space beneath the bridge, in an area divided in two by a full height glazed screen. A double deck has been created in the massive space, with a cherry clad mezzanine shaped like a hull containing Club Guastavino, a smaller, more exclusive restaurant and private dining room, floating under the bridge's vaults. Beneath the club is the main formal dining area, and below this a more informal brasserie.

The glass pavilion at Bridgemarket is an architectural element that serves as a kind of magnet. Much the same effect is achieved at Berns, Stockholm, a family of restaurants and bars in a converted nineteenth century concert hall next to the open spaces of Berzelli Park. Here, Conran & Partners worked with the building's ornate features, last extensively renovated in the 1980s to such splendour that it earned the nickname the "Gold Café", and included some contemporary additions. For instance, a new glass structure is added to the park elevation of the building of the former café to provide an entrance, vertical access and viewing point for the restaurants, terrace and conference facilities. Curved sheets of glass enclose a stainless steel and Jura limestone staircase, which in turn wraps around a lift core organising views of the restaurant at veranda level and then leads up to an open terrace. At night the glazed structure glows, revealing the activity inside. The project provided an opportunity to bring a large scale historic building back to life. These crisp, cool interventions do not blend in invisibly but make a bold contrast with the rich listed interiors, a place for stylish meetings within Stockholm, a city whose architecture is more often associated with 'rationalism' and 'social programming'.

Ariel view, Bridgemarket
59th Street Bridge
New York

View below the mezzanine
Guastavinos restaurant

Internal view
Guastavinos Restaurant
New York

New Conran Shop
Pavilion by night

Brand Values

Conran & Partners has had many opportunities to make an overtly aspirational statement for an interior –
an obviously heightened atmosphere being one tactic. The space for an aspiring brand is about persuading
the customer they are empowered, and does not necessarily need to employ precious or expensive
materials, as is demonstrated by the design for the department store Georges, in Melbourne, where it
was much more important for the practice to allow for the co-existence of diversity and coherence. Interior
design is too often used to spell 'old money' or aristocratic style, whether for genuine aristocrats or the
nouveau riche. The trend for brands like Gucci and Louis Vuitton to shake this rigidity in thinking, replacing
it with a much more ironic and playful deployment of signs of affluence, is a notable index of cultural change.
Conran & Partners work hard not to be formulaic, using art and photography to help give new dimensions
to a space's meaning. They also prefer a certain fluidity – in function, materials and circulation – for even a
heavily branded environment, marking out the design as tasteful without overwhelming the visitor.

Georges Department Store
Melbourne, Australia

following page   Perfume Department
Georges

Interior
Concorde Room, JFK
New York

The Concorde Room at John F Kennedy airport in New York, attempts to bring the 'image' of the airport lounge up to date, and is a good example of design that caters to rather than overwhelms the visitor. Whilst speed is the main reason for travelling by Concorde, on the ground there is the need for a space that is fresh, classical and relaxing, set away from the main airport environment. The choice of materials – travertine, green marble, walnut, oak, sycamore and marble mosaic – asserts a set of luxurious aesthetic values, with the many areas of the lounge varied so as to suit individual moods. A main axis comprising a wide walnut clad passageway, with business suite and facilities on either side – a passage emphasised at each end by two art works by Sol LeWitt. The main room of the lounge is designed around a collection of classic twentieth century furniture pieces, including works by Eileen Gray, Mies van der Rohe, Poul Kjaerholm, Eero Saarinen and Arne Jacobsen. Photographs by Eve Arnold are hung in the smoking room, and a mobile by Richard Smith shimmers behind etched glass panels that run the length of the space.

Fin de siecle to Twenty-first Century

In 1999, adopting the mantra of "no signature style but a partnership approach", Conran Studio and Sebastian Conran Associates merged with CD Partnership to become Conran & Partners. Since this merger a raft of new projects has continued the practice's expansion internationally, particularly in Japan, while new housing and urban developments now form a major part of its portfolio. New interiors for hotels, offices, the conversion of public buildings and exhibition design all add to this expansion. Even a small project, such as The Chef's Roof Kitchen Garden created for the annual Chelsea Flower Show in May 1999, typifies how architectural skills can be applied to the most modest of scales. Functioning as a structure and garden combined, it showcased Terence Conran's notion of the garden as an extension of the home – a glass enclosed kitchen jutting into a garden planted only with edible flowers and vegetables.

The idea of no signature style has been extremely helpful in responding to the explosion of interest in complex programmes with the need to create a sense of identity for a building that works on its own terms. The urban hotel as a contemporary type has commanded attention in this most recent phase of the practice's work, reflecting the growing fashion for design-led hotels and, more generally, design as a provider of cultural experience. Frequently, the concept for a hotel is that of a retreat, but one that must also provide a heightened experience of the city – drawing on its culture, and extending it so as to provide 'playgrounds' of facilities, not just for hotel occupants but also city dwellers. Myhotel, a town house hotel in London's Bloomsbury, completed in 1999, provides a strong conceptual example of this new type of hotel in central London, as does the transformation of the Great Eastern Hotel, the careful restoration of an enormous Victorian building. The Great Eastern Hotel manages to be understated and simple, but stylish at the same time. The sense of its vastness plays on the visitor, demanding fuller exploration.

The practice's most recent hotel project, the Park Hotel in Bangalore, India, provides a contrasting example of Conran & Partners' fusion of local influences with new technology in a city that is about to explode as India's Silicon Valley. The original 15 year old building was loosely influenced by the work of Le Corbusier, and its conversion provided an opportunity to evolve a modernist language across its exterior. Inside, this is brought into play with a contemporary design that uses a palette of Indian colours, local silks, materials and craft techniques to create an evocative, hybrid environment.

View of the Pavilion
Chelsea Flower Show

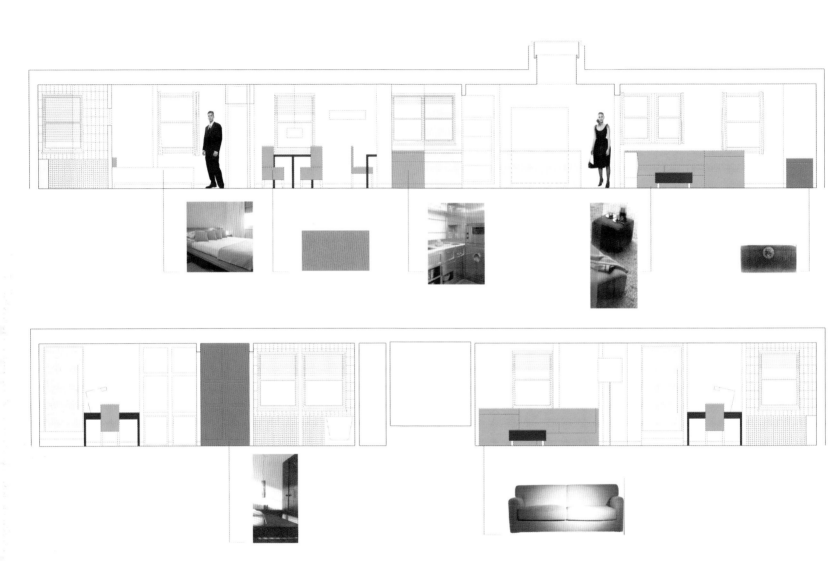

Penthouse   View of penthouse
Interior elevations
Myhotel

Urban Aspirations

The scale of Conran & Partners' urban regeneration work significantly expanded with Merchant Village in Glasgow – the practice's biggest project, and Ocean Terminal in Leith on the outskirts of Edinburgh, which opened in the autumn of 2001. Although Merchant Village has not yet been built, it drew on the practice's passion to build a large scale, complex project, encompassing a block and a half of city centre. The Merchant Village required working with listed buildings and designing substantial amounts of new construction for public and private spaces – apartments, shops, offices and a hotel. This experience is also reflected in the Metropolitan complex, a new entertainment and leisure facility, and another major work designed by the practice for the city of Glasgow.

While Metropolitan came through a competitive bid, Forth Ports approached the practice directly concerning the design of Ocean Terminal, one of Conran & Partners' largest completed projects to date. The brief was to create a new masterplan for an undeveloped waterside area at the heart of one of the city's brownfield site. Part of the regeneration of Edinburgh's harbour, as a residential, business and leisure quarter, it was a rare opportunity for Conran & Partners to develop Leith's identity as a new, exciting part of the city. It also provided the practice with the rare opportunity to express new thinking about the concept of the shopping centre – the resulting 100,000 square metre scheme, including shops, restaurants, cinemas, cafés and bars, allows for relaxing views of the city's largely undiscovered waterfront.

Japanese Trajectories

Towards the end of the 1990s, the practice began working on architectural and interior design commissions in Japan. The first Conran & Partners' project in the city was the Ark Hills Club in Roppongi, 1998, which brings together Eastern and Western eating and drinking spaces. Ark Hills Spa, 2000, a health club and bar within the Ark Hills complex, but with its own street entrance, uses simple materials, a stimulating use of orange and blue, and atmospheric lighting to create an inviting, almost domestic environment. The fresh approach here avoid both the clichéd pastel dominated design of many health farms as well as the utilitarian feel of the typical gymnasium.

These two projects add highly prestigious facilities to the Ark Hills building and plaza, a development with a bustling day and night life into which over 80 high quality eating, drinking and retail outlets are housed. They were followed by Kamiyamacho, a distinctive residential building in Tokyo for the Mori Building Company. Conran & Partners' involvement on key elements of Roppongi Hills, Tokyo, a 11 hectare site incorporating two 40 storey apartment towers, an 18 storey apartment hotel as well as retail and office buildings, further extends the practice's urban design agenda. This includes an acknowledged sense of common purpose and ambitions to build internationally at all scales.

The two 40 storey residential towers create high rise accommodation with a domestic scale and texture inside and out. A third building, Forest Hills Gate, a collaboration with Irie Miyake Architects, has a mixed use programme, with six floors of offices and five floors of apartments above, respectively reflected in the hybrid nature of the building's construction.

A current Japanese project, Roppongi Hills Club, due to open in the spring of 2003, has a highly original orbital layout. It is divided into numerous types of eating and drinking facilities, both public and private, according to a brief that asked for the visitor's experience to be one of constant change. The inner plan is circular, surrounded by four outer orbital zones extending on two sides into open plan spaces with views of Tokyo Bay and Shinjuku. At the same time the club's design manages to be consistent amidst all this diversity by being attentive to the ambience required of each space, whether crustacea restaurant, teppanyaki bar, cocktail lounge and library, or private dining room. It is this accepted sense of duality within Eastern culture that Conran & Partners have interpreted anew, drawing on the multi-disciplinary approach that exists in their own working methods and tastes.

The 21 year trajectory of the practice can be characterised as the finding of a freedom to explore its combined skills. Moving into larger urban projects only serves to reinforce the need to apply an inclusive, and at the same time individualised approach to context at all scales. Conran & Partners' ability to straddle social change, to adapt and find new ways of responding to the great variety of projects undertaken by the practice is part of its strength and prompts a closer analysis of the relationships they forge between theory and practice.

View through to
bedroom and bathroom

following pages   Pool
Ark Hills Spa
Tokyo

View along
relaxation corridor

Restaurant

THEORY &

The rational base of Conran & Partners' work is often complemented by their use of narrative, particularly in interior work. Narrative functions as a means to help open up ways of understanding how different design concepts, skills and materials might be used. Wood proposes a new axiom – "form follows fiction" – to replace, or at least supplement, the more familiar version of the Modern Movement mantra. This is pertinent to projects such as Lenbach in Munich, Das Triest in Vienna or the Fitzwilliam Hotel in Dublin. Undoubtedly, unfamiliar cultural contexts, combined with historical fabrics possessing a vivid previous life and in need of refurbishment, provide ample suggestions for new stories. It is creating a workable synergy between this and the overall brief that makes Conran & Partners' use of narrative effective. Told as a story, a number of complex meanings and orderings may be attached to a seemingly simple architectural idea. Narrative is only one tactic at Conran & Partners' disposal, however. Alongside this they maintain more conventional architectural aspirations, including a belief in materials and the way things are made; an interest in the way places are inhabited; and an enjoyment of bringing the traditions of modernism into dialogue with the local, the everyday and the decorative.

All the Directors at Conran & Partners place a high priority on architecture as a practice driven by ideas, an approach reinforced by a collective appreciation of difference, and the opportunities it affords. At various times, each undertook all or part of their architectural education at the Bartlett School of Architecture, and this has provided them with a common ground. At the same time, however, their individual architectural positions were marked by significant shifts in the School's approach to education from the 1980s to 90s – moving from a technologically determined modernist programme to a more "anything goes" eclectic approach to architecture. This background has, at least in part, informed the practice's adherence to both contemporary rational design and a commitment to narrative.

Conran & Partners' body of work emanates from a shared interest in the diversity of modern and contemporary European architecture, with such practitioners as Le Corbusier, Ludwig Mies van der Rohe and Louis Kahn embodying for the practice those qualities of formality, composition, clarity, proportion, materiality and refinement of detailing sought in their own work. Of more recent bearing, Paul Zara cites the "retentive crispnes" of the Swiss practice Diener & Diener, and the relatively austere projects of MacCreanor Lavington, as well as "the willful bravura" of Rem Koolhaas. And perhaps it is their own eclecticism Conran & Partners see mirrored in the work of Steven Holl, who is cited as an architect whose ideas and observations about a specific project condition allow him to generate a unique concept for each one.

Zara talks of an engagement with architectural language: "[our work is] moved both by the austere and the sensuous... finding solutions in many obscure and seemingly insignificant places, the quiet repetition in a polite 1950s civic building, subtly subverted by asymmetry, the marble linings in a window reveal of a 1960s high street bank, the quirky roof structure on an otherwise prosaic tower block, a barely indistinguishable change of direction in a long street elevation, the pop-out window high up on a 1960s department store. There is usually a reinterpretation of these in the architecture of the 1990s, but [we] prefer to look first to the source of an idea to see if it provides a clue to a contemporary solution."

Regarding the interplay between the rational and the narrative, Conran & Partners point out "a modernist can only do one building". A project such as Merchant Village could never have functioned on the basis of the "if you don't need it, get rid of it" approach. Rather it proposes multiple elevation treatments, each relating to its streetscape, allowing what is a mega-development to be given a more intimate scale. In a similar way, the multiple branding of spaces at the Great Eastern Hotel offers an episodic spatial composition that creates a distinct set of contrasting and yet complementary environments. The overtly self-conscious design of the Metropolitan, where the central space would be 'outside' or part of the public realm, crystallised the practice's stance.

Another feature of Conran & Partners' work is their consideration of surface. Wood notes that retail schemes invariably entail blank walls, and he cites Douglas Coupland, in *Generation X*, on the popular notion that "shopping centres exist on the insides only and have no exterior". This suspension of visual belief encourages shoppers to "pretend that the large, cement blocks thrust into their environment do not, in fact, exist". In contrast, Conran & Partners are conscious of both interior and exterior 'performance'. At Metropolitan, the mass of the cinema is articulated in an apparently rational/functional manner, but then the resulting 'pods' are each clad in a different material – pre-patinated copper, sandstone and zinc. This approach simultaneously roots the massive building to its immediate urban context, and subverts the apparent 'purity' of the architectural approach.

The practice's architectural approach cannot just be seen as the creative melding of a set of distinct interests shared by each Director, but a tactical intervention in urban contexts which are themselves highly heterogenous. Collaboration, both with team members and with clients, necessitates a healthy respect for difference, and allows the development of multiple, adaptive strategies capable of attending to the local, the everyday and even the decorative.

In taking objects and elements from one context and placing them in another, Soane refers to a process described by Levi-Strauss where it is possible to "create a dialogue between the traditional and the utopian". It's when the process of design does *not* appear to engage in any kind of theoretical discourse – defining the terms of a proposal and acknowledging the process of its engagement – that Conran & Partners believe architecture remains self-contained, autonomous, and removed from everyday life. The position subscribed to within the practice argues for the validity of a conceptual approach – not its mystification – and the certainty that a design has content and that this is not just an additional effect.

A narrative structure is useful as a method of combining theory and practice within a specific context. For Conran & Partners, creating narratives to help define spatial intentions drives the creative process, allowing for the use of metaphor as both a generative and communicative tool. Such a strategy also helps to engage every member of staff in the evaluation of a brief.

A singular method of practicing architecture is of limited use in the context of an ever-changing culture expressed in cycles of fashion and style, of which Conran & Partners' projects are clearly a part. An eclectic, non-dogmatic set of strategies is the best way to respond to an individual project, which, as the practice points out, has "its own set of criteria which are the result of the interaction between the circumstantial and the social". The mix of givens, such as the retaining of traditional features, with the need for decisive interventions in existing structures, helps to structure a path of lateral thinking. Consequently, by telling a series of stories and observations that lead to a design solution – by applying a 'meta-narrative' – results emerge that are hybrids of methods and ideas.

Interior architecture, in particular, requires an advanced ability to realise a client's desires at a micro-scale. This is a matter of interpreting and translating a mix of brief, site conditions, financial parameters and marketing profiles into something greater than the sum of its parts. The results of this approach can then not only stand up to the commercial imperatives of developers, but also make a distinctive identity for a newly created destination, as well as tapping into the public's impulses and interests. This, then, is a matter of branding, but also of communicating a range of inter-linked functions through a marriage of complementary skills.

Rather than creating a rigidly ordered 'kit of parts', designing for contemporary public spaces entails the successful interplay of a wide range of skills deployed across many disciplines. What enters the mix is adjusted according to the specific demands identified in a scheme. The following examples from Conran & Partners' work provide further insight into both narrative and spatial composition as complementary processes within architectural design.

Early photograph
Bluebird Garage
Kings Road, London

Bluebird, on London's King's Road, can be analysed in several ways. On the most obvious level, it engages its urban context in an understated yet powerful way. The refurbished forecourt, marked by modest but high quality paving and its steel and glass canopy, engages the passer-by. Its presence on the street is less suggestive than, say, the peepshow of the Rex Bar, but it still makes a statement. The architects also describe a narrative interplay between the suave luxury of the King's Road and the gutsy, prosaic history of the site. These find resonance in different elements of the brief – the courtyard with its fruit stall, the simple and undecorated food hall with its open ceilings and tiled floor set against the light airy restaurant and the luxury of the private Bluebird Club. The canopy on the forecourt develops this dichotomy in detail, with the concrete columns and galvanised steel structural members set-off by shiny, stainless-steel bolts and hanging rail.

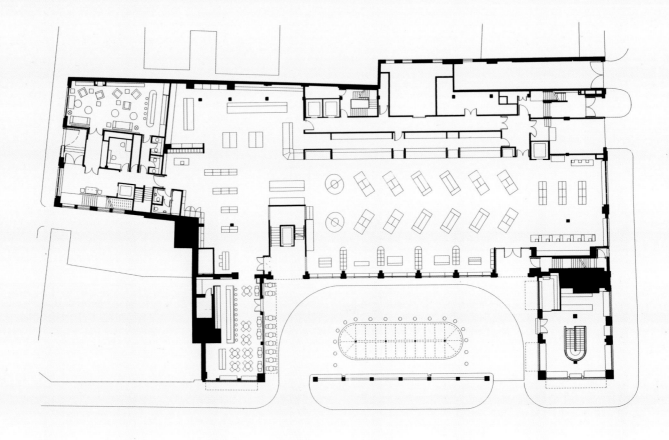

Ground floor plan   Views of forecourt
Bluebird   Bluebird

The forecourt is the first part of an entrance sequence to the main restaurant at first floor. The approach from the King's Road leads the visitor in a grand sweep up a new semi-external lift and stair to a first floor lobby space on the main axis of the dramatic roof structure. This has been partly closed in, to reduce the scale of the space and subvert its axial symmetry, focusing the restaurant back to the forecourt and Kings Road. This processional route draws the visitor in, and contrasts sharply to the entrance sequence of the Bluebird Club. From the pavement on Beaufort Street the visitor is forced through a series of right-angled turns, through a gated external lobby, entrance hall and staircase up to the two private dining rooms on the first floor. This contorted spatial sequence emphasises the air of exclusivity and privacy that the club presents.

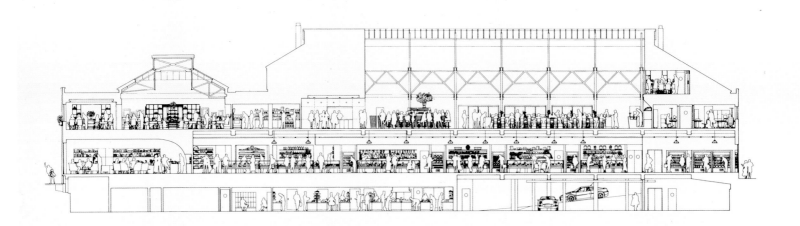

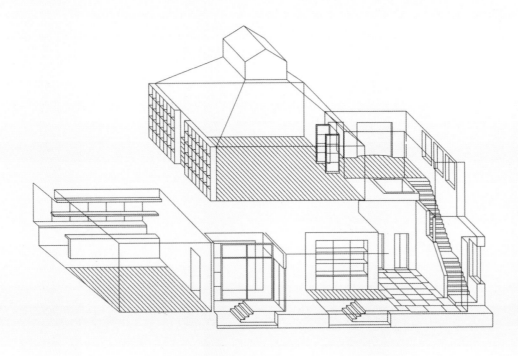

Long section showing
the Bluebird Store,
Restaurant, Kitchen and Club

Bluebird Club

The ornate/prosaic narrative is played out more subtly in the remodelling of the two sides elevations. On the Vale, with its service entrances and loading bay, galvanised glazing angles and zinc faced cladding panels mark the 'every day', in contrast to the brass and bronze used for the club entrance on Beaufort Street. Stepping into the Bluebird Club from the street feels like entering a villa. There is certainly an air of nostalgia – a homage to the almost mythical character Donald Campbell, whose 'Bluebird' cars and boats broke so many speed records in the 1920s and 30s. Furniture and fittings in solid oak and the imagery presented in paintings and photographs create a strongly impressionistic space, without falling into 'room set' scenography. As Isabel Allen has commented, "the practice's greatest coup is to have created interiors which look modern while hinting at a world that has evolved over generations of spilt brandy and stubbed cigars".

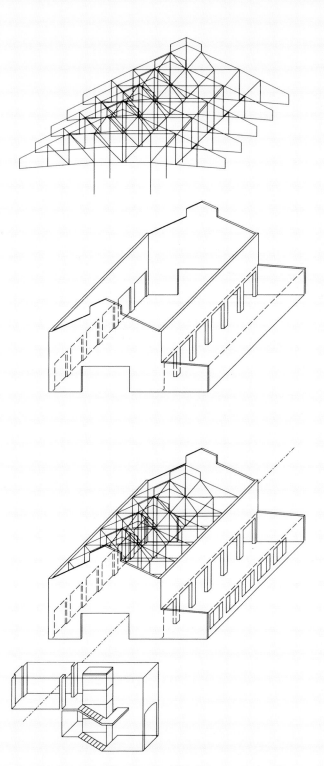

Bluebird Restaurant
Isometric Study

following pages   Bluebird Store   Bluebird Club   View of the Restaurant from the private dining room

Sometimes a basic and uncluttered formula is not enough and a particular area of an interior space requires a stronger narrative statement. The Das Triest Hotel offers a counterpoint to traditional Baroque with its open windows, long vistas and well considered details. Here Conran & Partners have made a set piece of the bar, with this room within a room contrasting with the rest of the hotel's design, a tactic used by the best hotels past and present. In this place of (usually) temporary occupation a heightening in atmosphere can be quite 'stage set' like. Dark and intimate, with timber walls and a silver ceiling, the bar contrasts with the rest of the building, with an entrance flanked by three alcoves reminiscent of railway compartments. Dubbed the "Silver Bar", it has echoes of the Viennese Adolf Loos' much earlier American Bar.

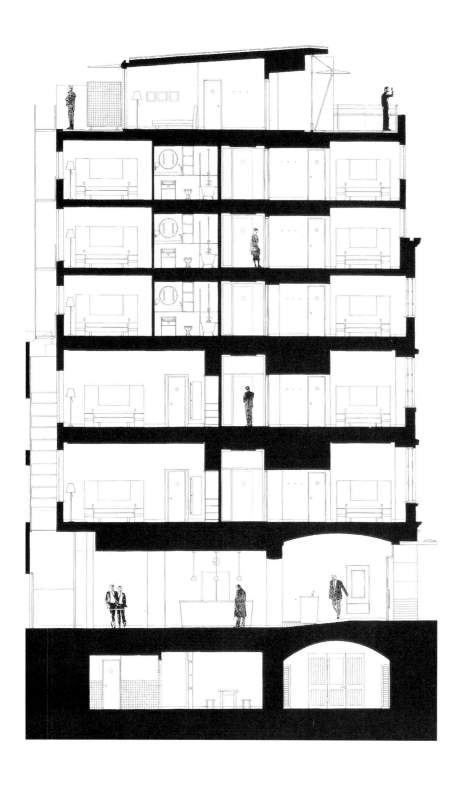

Cross section
Das Triest Hotel
Vienna

Interior view
Rex Bar
Iceland

At the Ark Hills Club in Roppongi, 1998 – a private members club with a collection of art works by Le Corbusier – the point of departure for the design was a reflection on Le Corbusier's belief in the plan being the generator of architecture. Here, the corridor is reinvented as the gallery, with Le Corbusier's work symbolising the dialogue between the occidental and the oriental. The planning of the spaces draws on this dynamic, with the Western dining areas pinwheelling around the more closely aligned Eastern dining areas, which include teppanyachi bars. The traditional forms of Japanese eating spaces have been tempered with a few innovative details – the blue glass front to the bar in the sushi restaurant suggests a fish tank, with the otherwise suede-clad walls providing a more generic sense of comfort. The gallery space connects the two, while the core of the club is its reception area, which serves as a gathering place for the lounge. Many of Le Corbusier's works are a highly condensed abstraction of three dimensional experience as well as being visions of the world represented: this intensity of means has influenced Conran & Partners in making a hybrid identity for the club, between local and global, and traditional and contemporary culture.

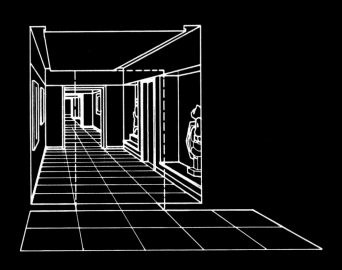

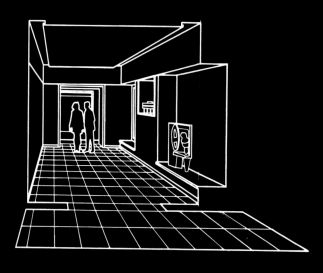

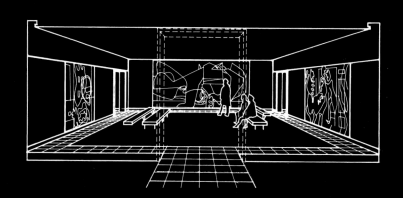

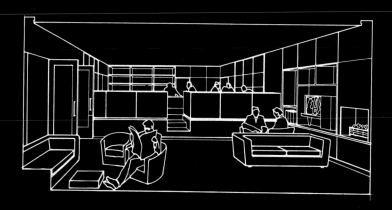

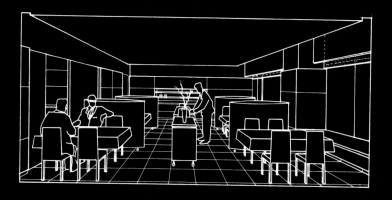

Top clockwise
Ark Hills Club

Tepanyaki   Gallery   Private Dining   View from gallery

It is important that a thematic does not become trapped in a historical language. At the Fitzwilliam Hotel in Dublin, Soane coined the phrase "Baronial Moderne" to capture the spirit of the past blended with the present, as well as combining a sense of town and country. This approach suited the setting on St Stephens Green, a verdant square in the centre of the city, where the client wanted to open a contemporary five star hotel equal to its continental counterparts.

The baronial collage that resulted was sophisticated, but could easily have remained a pseudo-historical backdrop. The tactile use of materials and plain bold colours: black and white marble, green Barcelona limestone, polished stainless steel and American walnut, mitigates against this kind of cultural referencing becoming overpowering. The textured palette of materials is tempered by clean lines, with contrast in the light and airy guest rooms between the rich dark wood, simple off-white walls and flowing curtains. The bedrooms continue the narrative, playing up the character of the country house without becoming too eccentric. The tall bed head – a walnut frame surrounding a crisp linen embroidered hanging – dominates the room. Facing the bed is a desk with a voyeuristic glass topped drawer. The rooms open off the main hall via a stone clad 'keep' with a glass 'drawbridge' connecting the mezzanine to the staircase leading outside. A walnut wall curves around from the keep to enclose the reception desk, behind which hangs a large artwork creating a heraldic backdrop. As such, Fitzwilliam asserts itself as running against the grain of the large multi-national hotels of the past two decades.

Lobby
Fitzwilliam Hotel
Dublin

The most explicit and wilful application of the narrative approach was perhaps in Conran & Partners' proposal for Lenbach – a restaurant and bar inserted into the listed interior of a nineteenth century Munich palace.

Creating a narrative based on the medieval concept of the Seven Deadly Sins, a concept fitting both the history of the building and its decadent *fin de siècle* atmosphere, the practice set about making the idea work in physical terms. The classical axis becomes a processional space, and the opaque glass balustrade of the upper gallery a screen for projected images. The basement foyer and rest rooms have been conceived as an imaginary prison, with rough slate floors, red plaster walls and zinc and stainless steel doors and fittings. The project necessitated a team not just of architects and interior and lighting designers, but also graphic designers, artists and craftsmen. It could be described as a cathartic design – one making sense of the client's request to link all of the elements using the equivalent of an operatic leitmotif. But, of course, there is a fine line between drama and melodrama, both in design and musical productions. Here, on the contrary, the focus was on the creation of something appropriate for an ideal, informal, twenty-first century café society.

One major area of the practice's work in which the idea of the narrative thread is vital is in the treatment of existing historic fabric that has to be both revitalised and set in a contemporary design context. The sheer scale of the Great Eastern Hotel, a building dating from the turn of the century, made it the practice's largest interiors project in London. A sense of the drama and glamour of the original had to be maintained in the doubling of the hotel's volume, with the incorporatation of over 267 bedrooms and six restaurants. Many of the Great Eastern Hotel's idiosyncratic, listed architectural features had to be restored but also set in a contemporary context. The Manser practice designed the central atrium for the clients, while Conran & Partners "evolved everything you see and feel", creating a meta-narrative that made sense of a widely disparate set of formal and spatial elements. The result is a collage, and as at the Fitzwilliam this is done with a knowing sense of history. Multiple branding is a key feature of the project, with the fragmentation being deliberate and desirable; with surprises in the way the spaces are hemmed together and given an overall coherence.

The building's proximity to the busy Liverpool Street railway terminal provide the practice with a cue, suggesting an atmosphere in which a sense of movement and a feeling of repose are equally strong. The unmistakable feel of grandiose classicism in the foyer, for instance, with its slightly funereal black marble, is underscored by its impression of being a runway, a wide open space that the visitor has access to and can move along into the rest of the building. Allied with an adjoining 'cigar box' style lounge space walled in crown-cut timber is a small library with contemporary classic furniture pieces by Charles and Ray Eames and Mies van der Rohe. The impression one is given by the Great Eastern Hotel is of a studied classicism, where an understanding of historical and contemporary elements combine.

Lenbach Restaurant
Munich

following pages
Great Eastern Hotel

Reception   Atrium   Main
entrance

Atrium   View through
circular bedroom
window

Typical
new bedroom

Miyabi
Japanese
Restaurant

Aurora
Restaurant

In restructuring a building its history needs to be peeled back. If this is not possible internally, more flexible elements can be introduced to alter its spatial experience. With a project such as the creation of a restaurant and café in the Florence Hall of the Royal Institute of British Architects, mobile elements have been used to make the space flexible, and one in which exhibitions can also be shown. A row of semi-circular banquettes form a permeable scalloped edge between the aisles of the café and the exhibition space. On wheels, these can be turned around to transform the centre of the hall into an events area.

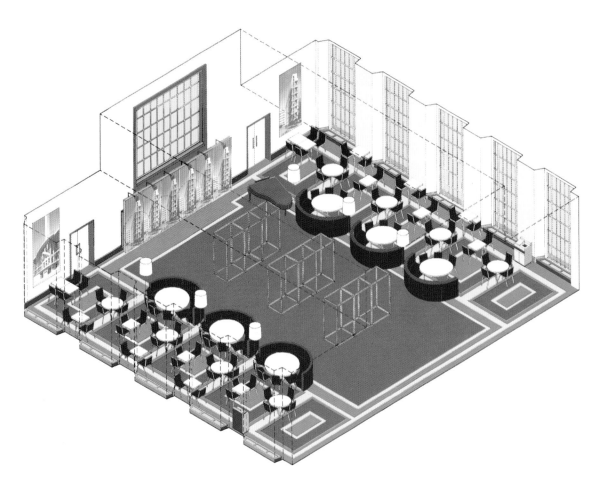

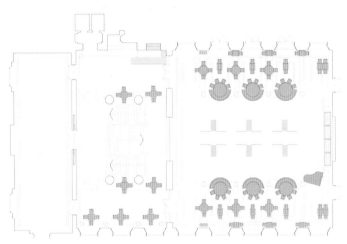

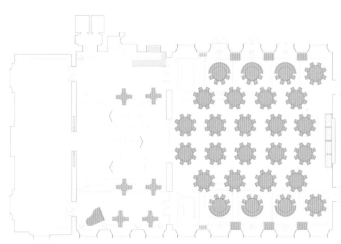

Isometric
Florence Hall

Layout options
Florence Hall

Florence Hall
Royal Institute of
British Architects

The integration of imported and local elements in a project is about creating a sufficiently strong framework for expression. The Park Hotel in Bangalore, India, is a good example of a refurbishment producing a lively, contemporary and locally embedded cultural statement. Converted from a three star hotel into a 'boutique' hotel, the building uses Indian craftwork and colours to create a hybrid and sensual environment to meet a brief for an 'urban resort'. A simple four-storey concrete-framed structure, it was built as a budget hotel 15 years ago, along the lines of a loose reading of Le Corbusier's work in India. A very simple, austere and flexible conversion, the building is now whitewashed and marked by ziggurat-like balconies. The existing Indian features on the façade were removed and only the reveals of the windows, painted in bright colours, hint at a contained richness within. The surrounding landscape, remodelled with granite sets, adds to the heightened presence of the conversion. An element of *tromp l'oeil* – a new canopy made from painted concrete looking like a large piece of furniture sitting on the stone – playfully extends this language.

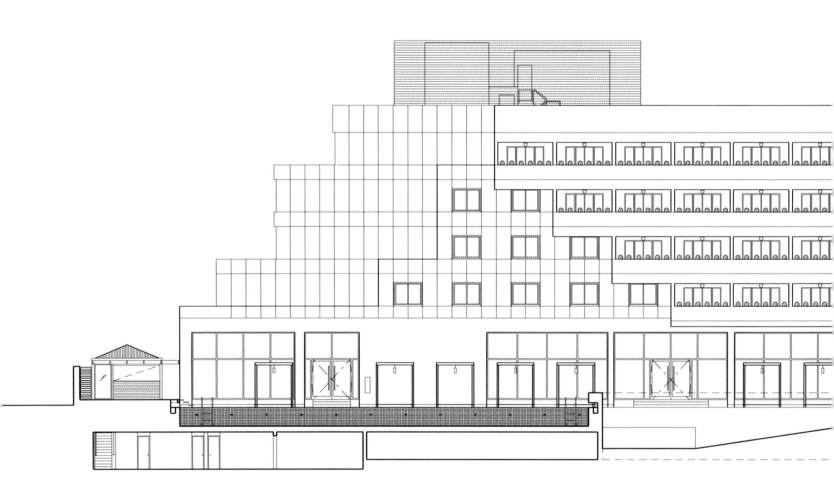

Park Hotel
Bangalore

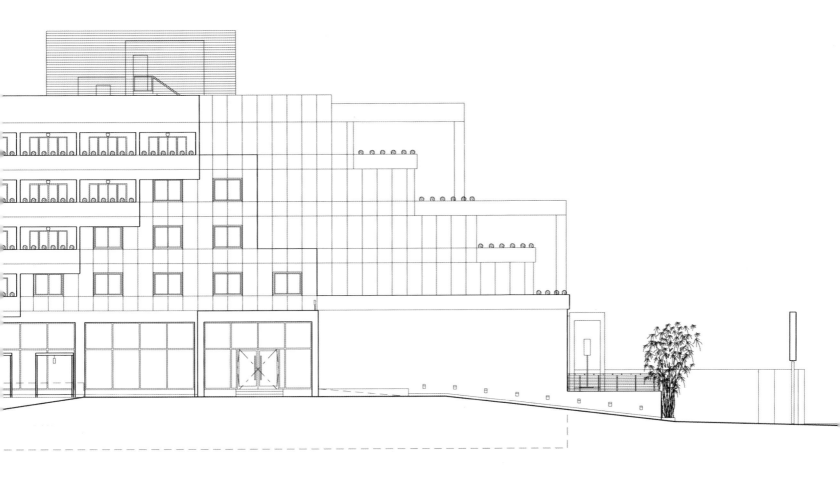

The main lobby, a huge sky blue curtained space, is linked to the rest of the ground floor by a vista of marble clad openings which create a perspectival grand axis, leading off to a banqueting room, coffee shop, library, restaurant and bar. Conran & Partners' desire to create a fusion between the craft and colour of traditional India and the area's technological development reaches a high point in the I-Bar. Here, low tables and chairs are scattered on a rich woven carpet of a complex 'silicon chip' pattern. The walls are 'soft' up to the height of the bar, which is not only designed as a glowing surface, but is slightly canted within the space to suggest movement and an environment in flux. The flickering images from a line of small flat television screens above the bar create a complementary sense of constant change. Next to a pool tiled in vivid blue ceramic, separated from the hotel by a terrace, is a pavilion and regimented row of simple timber gazebos, visible through large windows in the lobby. This is more West Coast in feel, adding to the sense that the treatment of the overall hotel environment is one of a collage of styles and influences.

Projects like the Park Hotel show the practice's interest in using a matrix of references – both contemporary and historic–which can be brought together to form a new entity. The practice does not invent an entire architectural aesthetic; rather their environments, whilst still expressive for those occupying them, are much more in keeping with each particular context. This open-endedness in creative protocol was extended to the Park Hotel's furniture, which had to be designed in its entirety as ready-made furniture could not be imported. Several original decorative strategies and juxtapositions of materials are deployed, at times almost willfully collaging different styles and expressions to create a sense of the theatrical. These designs frequently engage with new technology to combine experiential effects with a crafted layering of geometric decoration.

As with their approach to craft processes, Conran & Partners' concept of landscape design is a way of seeing how the surrounding environment can play a creative role in a project. The design of the Niki Club explicitly encourages the guest to interact with the landscape. The layout of the site, states Soane, "is based on a fragmented grid which is understood as a memory of the city, with interventions in the landscape mediating between the urban condition and nature". The lodge building is a horizontal slab, housing the reception area and the main glass enclosed dining room. There is a spa below, reached by an external stair passing through a small well lit courtyard. The rest of the accommodation is away from the main building, with paths leading to 20 timber-clad pavilions. The journey is intended to be part of the experience of staying here – a kind of adventure or safari, with the pavilions grouped around a formal garden.

Façade detail
Park Hotel
Bangalore

Top left clockwise
Park Hotel
Bangalore, India

Main entrance
at night

Views of
entrance and
poolside

Lift lobby

View along
ground floor
internal street

Bar

Top left
clockwise

Main
reception

Detail of hand
carved column
within the lobby

Bedroom
balcony detail

View of suite
bedroom

Detail of
Monsoon
restaurant

View along
corridor

Monsoon
restaurant

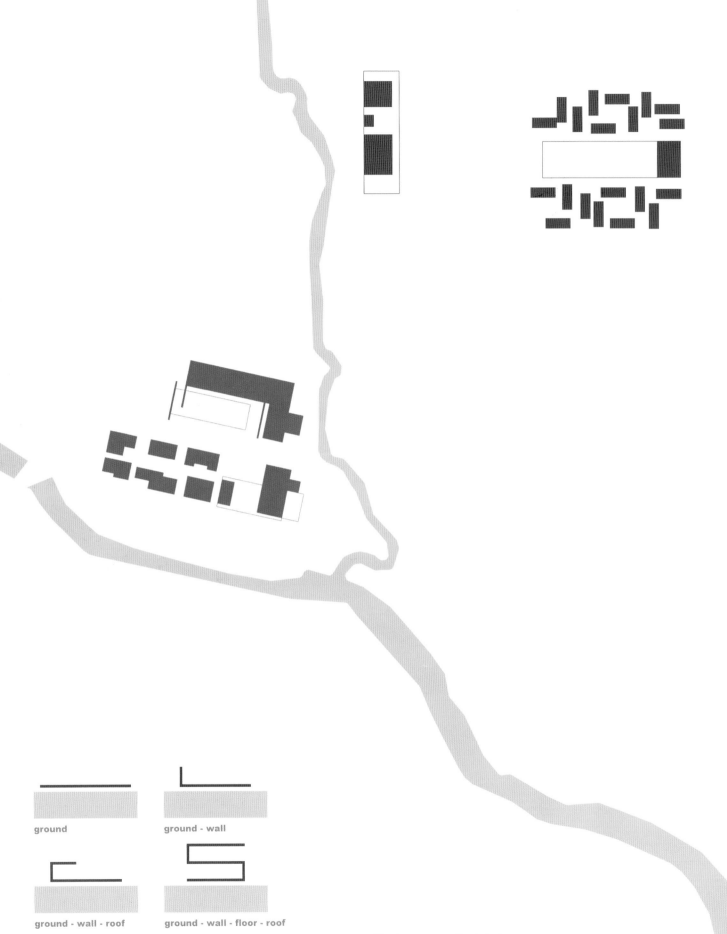

ground

ground - wall

ground - wall - roof

ground - wall - floor - roof

Site plan
Niki Club
Nassu, Japan

Typological
diagrams,
Niki Club

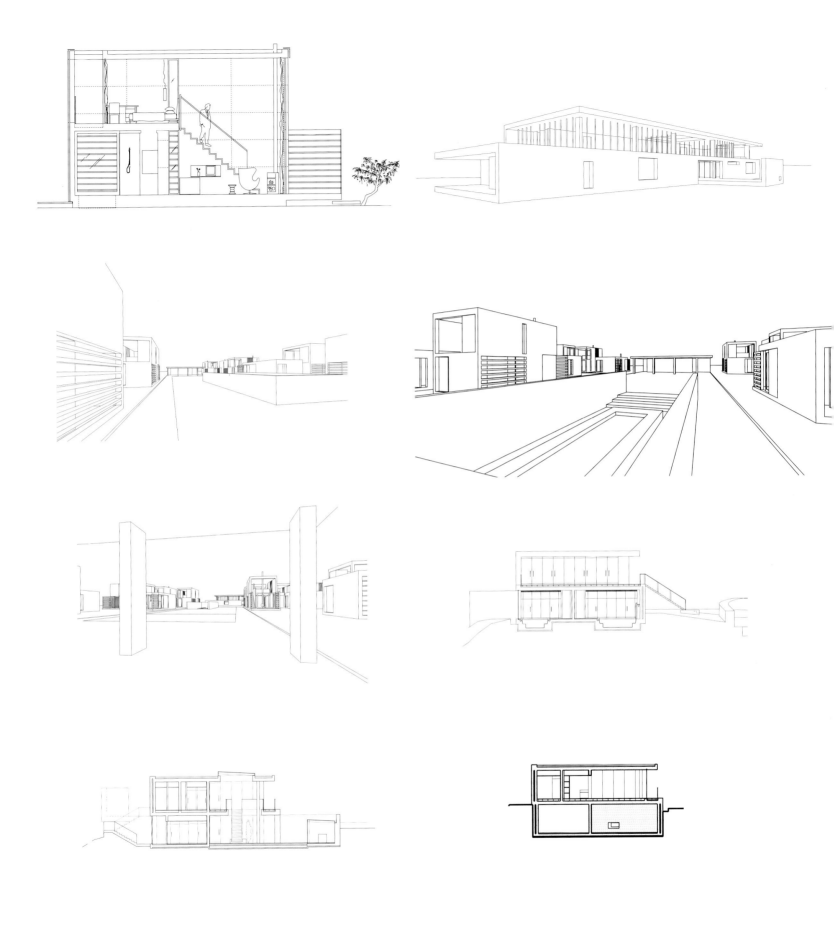

Top left to
bottom right

Cross-section
through pavilion

View of
main building

View of
pavilions

View of
communal
zone

View from
main building

Section
through
Spa

Section
through
courtyard

Section
through
reception

Given Conran & Partners' conscious use of narrative as a design tool, it is perhaps not surprising that they have also established a reputation in the field of exhibition design, where there is an overt and didactic relationship between architectural form and cultural content. For *From the Bomb to the Beatles, 1945-65*, 1999, commissioned by the Imperial War Museum, Conran & Partners worked on the theme of Post War culture using the medium of collage, with the resultant sequence of spaces, including room sets, shaping the progress from austerity to affluence. A dark and threatening room dedicated to nuclear war creates an emotional twist in the tale here, and contrasts with the stability of the exhibitions final room, which shows how the baby boom generation has grown up.

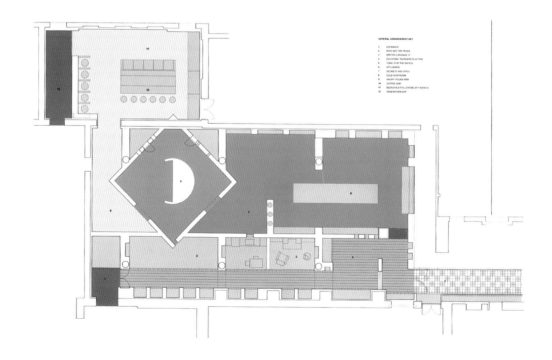

Collages exploring four thematics
From the Bomb to the Beatles, 1945-65
Imperial War Museum, London

Plan of exhibition

View of
'Bomb Room'

The exhibition *London Eats Out* for the Museum of London, 1999, straddled five centuries, showing how many aspects of late twentieth century dining trends have, in fact, had a very long history. Pavilions, each clad in a different material representing different historical building typologies, were strung along a horizon line of information, objects and themes. The project encouraged the visitor to discover the connections between different periods and experiences and questioned the belief that social histories are simply linear.

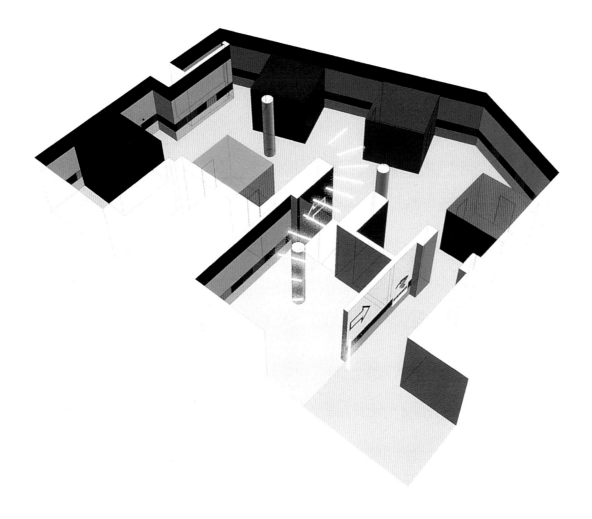

London Eats Out
Aerial perspective
Museum of London

Display case and
exhibition graphics
Museum of London

EATING OUT IN LONDON
THEN + NOW

In 1815 the first London restaurant guide, *The Epicure's Almanack*, recommended just 464 eating places in London. The 1999 equivalent, *Harden's London Restaurants*, recommends over 1200 and they are clustered in London's wealthy and commercial areas.

19th

20th

The idea of public space as a purely public funded phenomenon is becoming increasingly rare in industrialised cities and is better understood as an interweaving of private-public initiatives. Environments designated as commercial or private space, especially those with an anachronistic function like small-scale industry, are being rapidly reinvented for play rather than work. Through a combination of regeneration and urban planning, a new political dynamic has come to drive urban development and there is a growing concern for the quality of public spaces. This extends to interiors as well as exterior environments, a trend strongly reflected in the commissioning of public interior projects which radically force change upon a street, inserting a popular and recognisable brand where previously there was little life at all. Such developments have the effect of blurring the distinction between types and uses of space and the advertising – hoardings that intervene between them. This also acts as a catalyst for ancillary commercial growth, which then creates new demands – for parking to be rethought, housing provision to be upgraded and streets to be widened and improved.

A new enthusiasm for high quality urban living has also contributed here. In the UK, central government's eagerness to address this issue has been channelled through initiatives like the Urban Task Force Report, and the establishment of CABE (Commission for Architecture and the Built Environment), set up in 1999 to act as its champion for design quality in buildings, spaces and places across England. Challenges within the built environment include not only improving the interface between the design and construction process, but also encourage a high level of procurement and the development of new buildings and urban spaces through competitions and the media.

Merchant Village Site
Merchant City
Glasgow

How, then, do we characterise Conran & Partners' larger, more complex projects? Merchant Village and the Metropolitan building, both for Glasgow, and Ocean Terminal, Edinburgh, are three of the the practice's major commissions of the last few years. More than just public facilities, they represent the clustering of functions into a diverse set of interlinked environments.

The unrealised Metropolitan was one of several examples of a new building type (the urban entertainment centre or UEC) developed in the early 1990s typified by Manchester's Printworks, O_2 in London and the Corner House in Nottingham. These massive cinema-anchored leisure developments and food complexes attempt to bring the advantages of out-of-town leisure developments to city centre locations. The semi-public developer-controlled interior spaces provide safe alternatives to 'real' city-street night-life.

Conran & Partners envisaged Metropolitan's central mall space as a covered external space, reminiscent of unrealised proposals by Alexander "Greek" Thompson for a glazed residential street. The different cladding materials for the giant cinema 'pods' were to be carried through to the mall space, emphasising its reading as a covered courtyard, part of the public realm, rather than an internalised and private 'themed' environment, cut off from the city. In fact, the client eventually insisted on a fully themed approach and others were appointed to develop proposals for this – based on the 'industrial heritage' of the Clyde, complete with girders, cranes and glowing smelters.

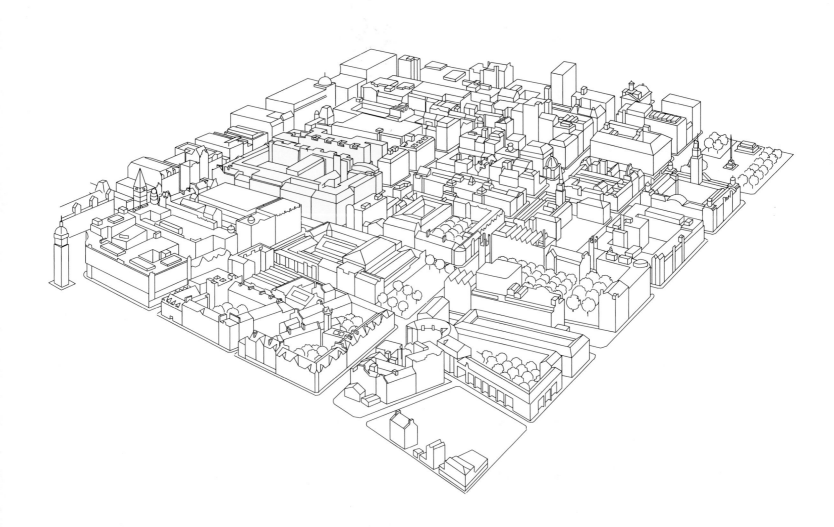

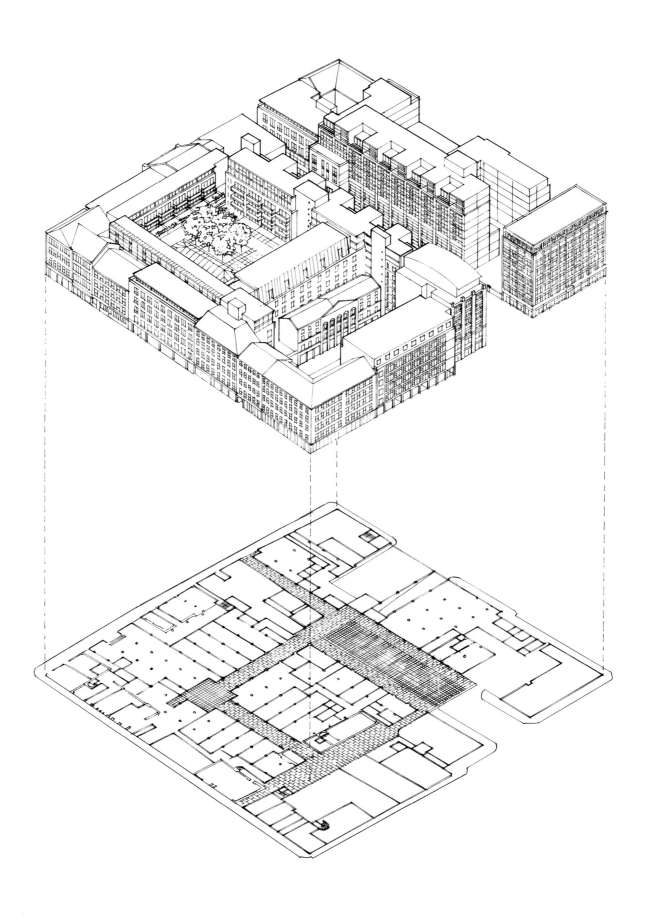

Merchant Village
Isometric

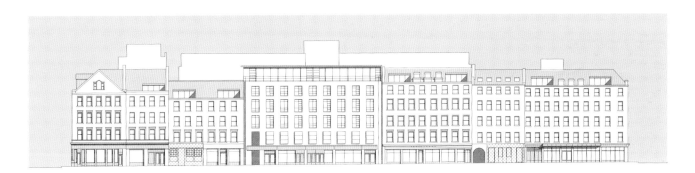

Merchant Village
Street elevations

Metropolitan
View of model from south east
showing car park

The treatment of the streetscape around the Metropolitan shows how Conran & Partners' approach to an urban context has evolved. The confrontation between the building and city grids creates a series of stepped returns along Osborne Street to the north and Howard Street to the south. This 'layering' has the effect of breaking down the perspective of the streetscape, through a picturesque device strengthened by the different cladding materials. The Metropolitan's façade also shows how Conran & Partners' have learnt new ways of enhancing the potential of the main elevation of a building beyond a conventional architectural language. The car park, with its large projection screens and poster sites, is aligned with 'folded' panels. Horizontal strips of metal meshes, louvres and perforated planes give this a tough, striking appearance.

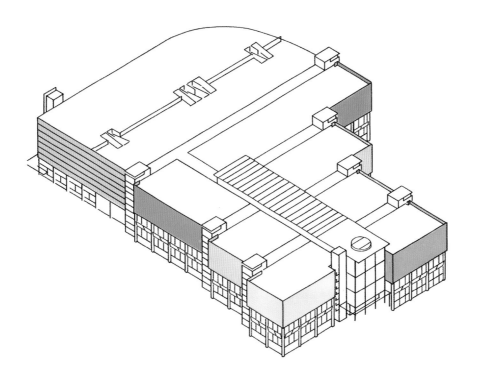

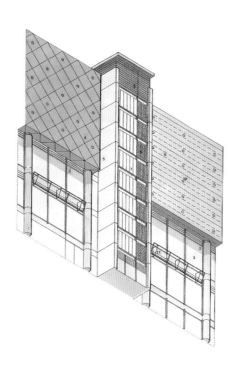

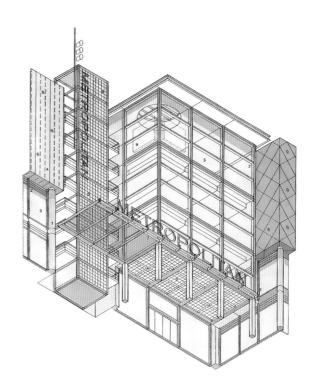

Massing/elevation
daigram

Up-isometric
elevation studies

The UK is now accustomed to increasing numbers of 'mega' shopping centre facilities, such as Lakeside at Thurrock and Bluewater. For the most part, these create space within their limits rather than connecting their facilities to the city through a reviving of its historic fabric. The challenge of responding to developers' sophisticated visions for contemporary public spaces, and designing to satisfy both the microcosmic and macrocosmic dimensions given such a context, necessitates a multi-disciplinary approach. Above all, it requires an understanding of how design can shape an environment of varied social experiences that is genuinely part of the city and embraces rather than rejects or replaces the urban street. Shopping centres, in particular, are frequently internalised in composition, but Conran & Partners provide an outward looking perspective, making public spaces that are flowing and convivial, rather than hyper-designed and inward looking. This is an aesthetic stance that incorporates a strong sensitivity towards a coherent sense of place but also the quality of life on the street. Ocean Terminal is at the heart of a major masterplanning and regeneration scheme the practice has been involved with on Edinburgh's waterfront area since 1995. Set on the side of the docks in Leith, it includes Granton harbour and the Newhaven peninsular. Conran & Partners were initially asked to design the Royal Yacht Britannia Visitor Centre on the site, which opened to the public in 1999. In tandem with this the client, Forth Ports, invited a second commission for a retail and leisure complex, 400 metres in length, for the same waterside location. The masterplan area is 10 to 15 minutes drive from Princes Street in the city centre, and comprises a mix of maritime heritage architecture and new buildings. Forth Ports, led by Terry Smith, its Chief Executive, were keen to create a new environment that would enter the popular imagination as a piece of the city, to create a little bit of Sydney Opera House 'pizzazz' on home ground.

The 'Leith boom', as it has become known, was initiated before Forth Port's huge investment in the shopping centre, by the securing of the area as a location for Britannia. Now, new apartment buildings and converted listed buildings at Commercial Quay are driving the area's transition into a working waterside environment, joining existing facilities, such as the stylish Malmaison Hotel and the extensive Scottish Executive offices. Remaining stretches of land are being attended to one by one, so that redundant maritime elements and dockside areas are transformed and incorporated within the city.

Ocean Terminal presented a rare opportunity for the practice, relatively inexperienced in schemes of this scale and type, to express a new way of dealing with such a project, particularly given a site by the water where openness to the surrounding environment was essential. It sits parallel to the quayside on the Western Harbour, where from the second floor level (cinema, restaurant and leisure units) there are spectacular views out across the estuary to the hills of Fife and back towards the skyline of Edinburgh. The brief was for a mixed use building, including a cinema complex, and called for a series of dramatic internal spaces, including a three storey rotunda and a grand hall overlooking the water. Conran & Partners' role at Ocean Terminal was to design the whole building and fit out the common internal spaces. Some of the units are for Conran Restaurants and include a branch of the Zinc Bar and Grill and a brasserie overlooking the Visitor Centre. The interior design includes a food terrace, an enormous glazed space at the heart of the building at first floor level, which captures dramatic views out across the Western Harbour.

1995 aerial photo
Leith Docks

Outside, the three storey, steel framed building is clad in terracotta tiles, granite and cast stone – all materials that will mellow with age. Inside, French limestone and wood floors contribute a sensuous feel to the centre's spatial ambience. Ease of circulation, a constant problem given anything coming into the category of 'mega' and mixed use – due to the sheer scale and complexity of user patterns – was vital. Making the shopping centre an internally oriented, compartmentalising space would have been a waste of its rich location. Instead the building is a rigid architectural box with views adding to the sense of spaciousness and tactility provided through the buildings detailing. The building's views can be seen as an antidote to what Michael Wilford refers to as "museum fatigue", providing a sense of relaxation after the bustle of the main shopping area. This approach is in stark contrast to the typical internalised shopping centre, such as Meadowhall, Sheffield.

Between 1995 and 1999, the practice developed three quite different schemes for the site. All had a very similar brief, but each was, as Conran & Partners admit, more efficient and realistic than its predecessor. Much of what has gone into the finished building is familiar to other shopping centres, but it is clear that the lateral thinking that informed the original proposal allowed some unusual features to survive the inevitable process of rationalisation. Firstly, it has more than the two levels characteristic of most buildings of this type, as well as a unique roof-top viewing gallery. In Scotland only the Lighthouse in Glasgow, converted by Page & Park, and the new Museum of Scotland in Edinburgh, by Benson & Forsyth, offer this kind of contemporary precedent. The 'footfall' at Ocean Terminal's upper level is sustained by the cinema, the draw of Britannia (it received 400,000 visitors in its first year) and multi-level parking. Not only does it have a relatively low proportion of retail units, offset, in part, by these other attractions, but the mall itself is straight, free of pop-outs or 45° splays, relieved by the careful siting of the rotunda and first floor hall.

The building has a horizontal, layered composition that responds to its location, engaging the open landscape of the port area. The building is composed as a long, low and pure shape – a primary volume like the hull of a vessel – with the rotunda, hall and cinema reading as superstructures. Inside, at each level, timber floors, canvas drapes and horizontal balustrades make further subtle reference to the great cruise liners that visited the port in its heyday. What makes Ocean Terminal a convincingly contemporary building is that it deals with issues of history and context without resorting to overt 'theming'. In terms of its significance as an urban facility, the project is the largest shopping centre and leisure development in Edinburgh, making up for the lack of comparable leisure and retail facilities in the north of the city. It also attracts people from a regional catchment area covering the entirety of East Central Scotland, including Fife, the Borders and the Central Belt. It is easy to scorn the out or edge of town shopping centre as an idea, but harder to make a convincing destination out of redundant land.

These three projects join a body of work that includes Conran & Partners' other large scale urban developments, such as Bridgemarket, Butlers Wharf and Bluebird. It is a sector that is likely to grow, with future prospects for the practice taking shape in Guildford and Leeds. Urban schemes on this scale demand communication as well as organisational qualities, and an understanding of how to intervene in existing, inevitably historical contexts. The public realm is reinventing itself daily and perceptions of time, place and space have shifted ground. Architecture cannot overlook such matters. It has to be at the centre of this organic process. The question is, given this, what are the most effective strategies?

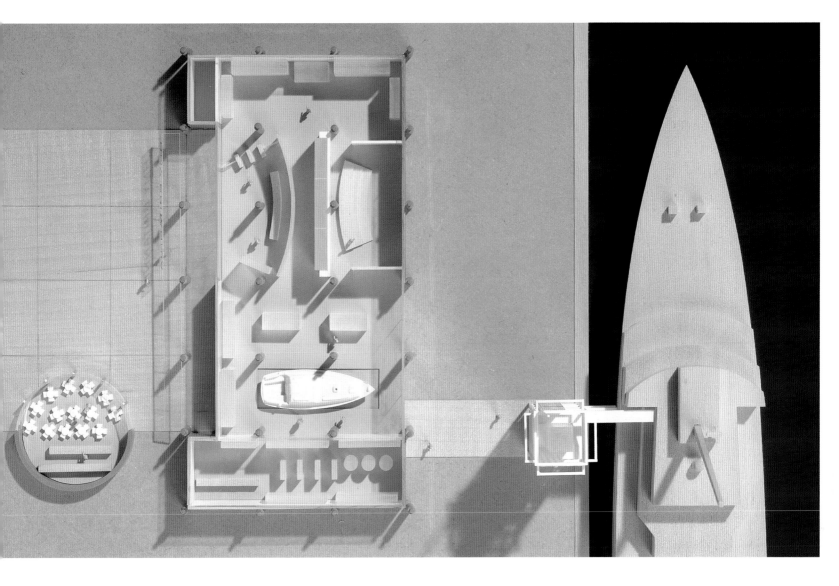

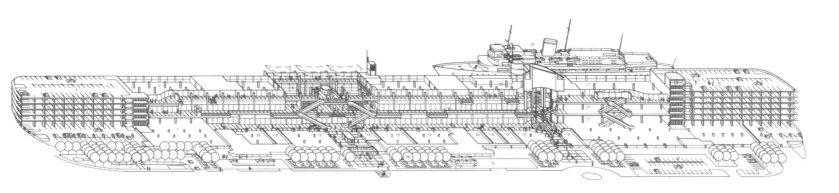

Ocean Terminal
Britannia Interim
Visitor Centre model

Cutaway
isometric

following pages

Ocean Terminal
master plan area

Ocean Terminal
Original (1995)
scheme model

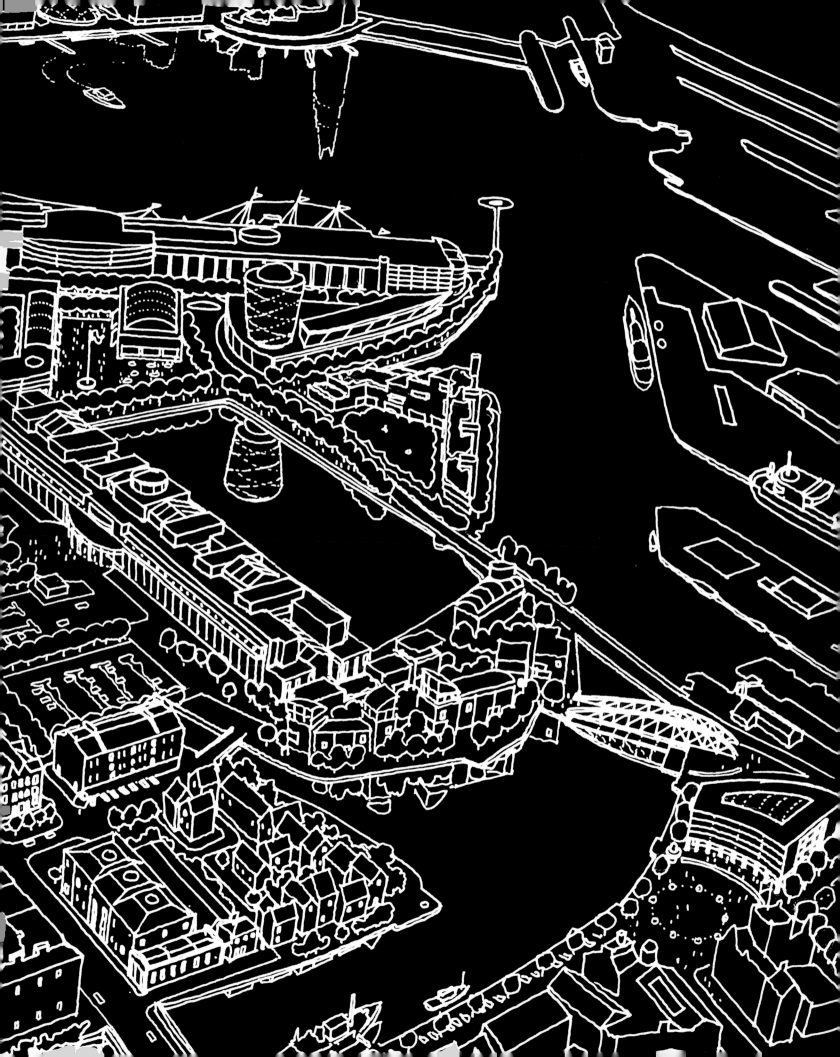

OCEAN TERMINAL 09/09/27

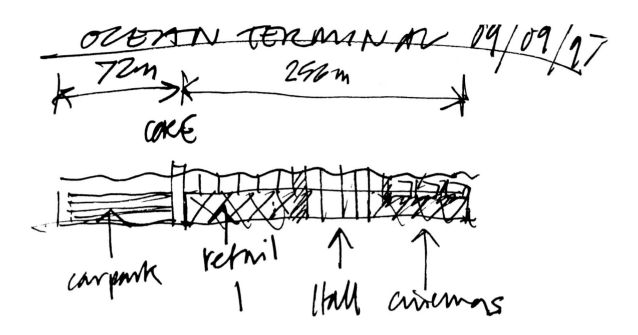

72m — CORE — 256m

carpark   retail   Hall   cinemas

*new concept: different objects
under a big, simple roof.

Ocean Terminal
Development sketches

LIVING

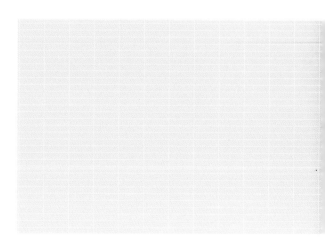

Over the last 20 years the design of domestic living spaces across the globe has been affected at every level by changing lifestyles in metropolitan areas. The diversification of the types of groups constituting an individual household, the blending of work and play and the growing interest in open-plan living in loft and loft-style developments have led to increasingly hybrid and versatile solutions. Individuals' desires for a home that is both a sanctuary and a place of self-expression have led to much higher standards of layouts, and the use of fitted elements and appliances, all of which are more likely to be frequently updated. Fashion has invaded the home, and nomadic living has outpaced the desire for long lasting formal statements. At the recent international Archilab architectural conference and exhibition on housing in Orléans in June 2001, the curators concluded that housing design needs to reflect individual and collective desires, use innovative techniques to reply to standardisation, and in order to reflect changing living patterns, be informal and interactive.

Part elevation
Roppongi Hills
Tokyo

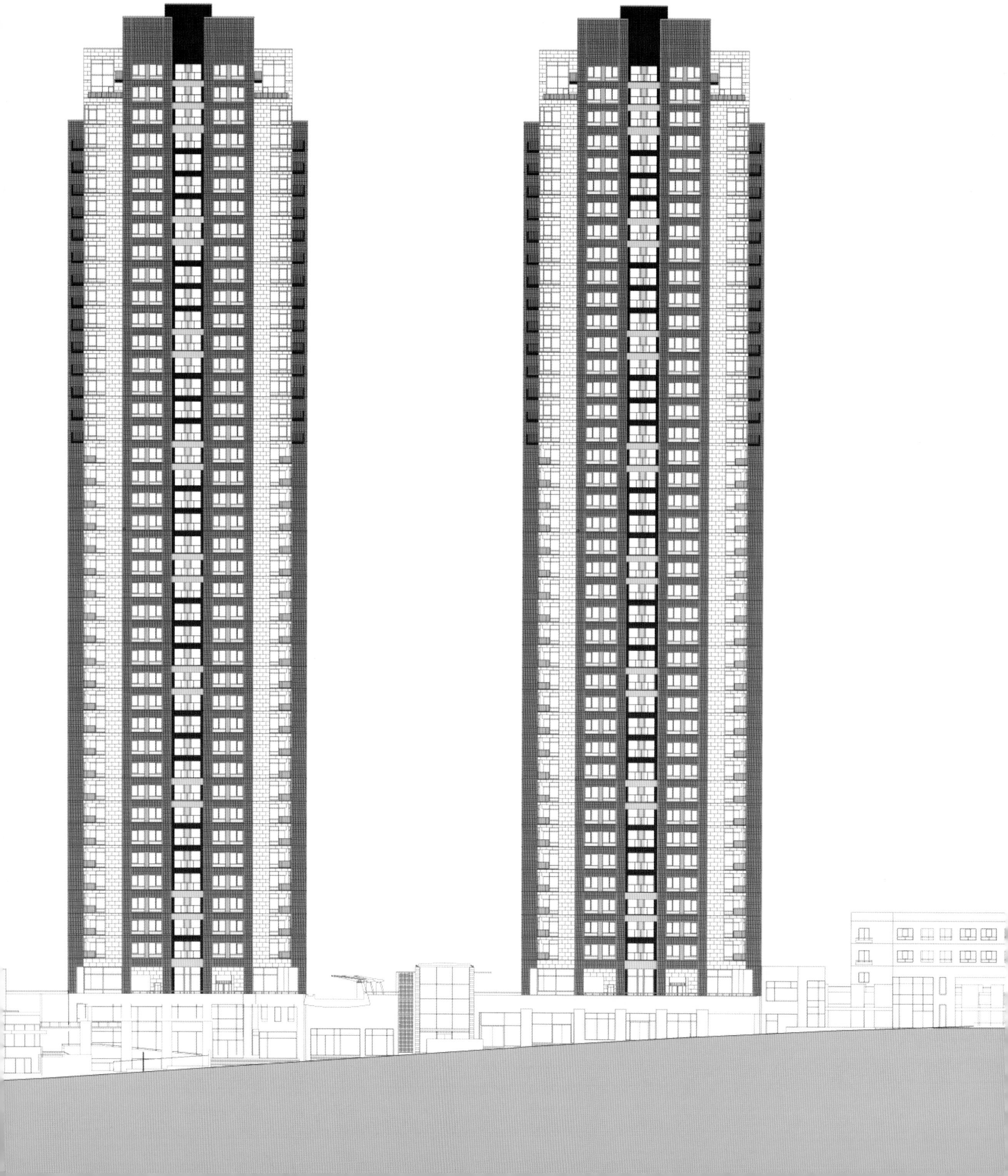

Work on projects in Japan for Mori soon led to Conran & Partners being invited to design a unique low-rise apartment building in a central residential area of Tokyo. Kamiyamacho, or 'Forest Terrace Shoto', as the Mori Building Company call it, is a four storey 'neighbourhood building' in the area of Forest Hills. Off the main street, just ten minutes walk from Yoyogi Park, the area is quiet and secluded. Designed to house a number of different domestic environments across the site, the building has a strong corner angle, which dominates the initial view of the development. Its modest size is deceptive, with the façade layered in rustic brown, green and cream. A green patinated copper shield contains the bedrooms, with a limestone clad box holding the kitchens and vertical circulation, and a steel framed block with timber infill panels defining the main living spaces. The layers step back to include a row of gardens at the rear of the ground floor flats. Inside, a spacious lobby with a stone water feature, a slate topped reception desk and seating – echoing the generosity of the living spaces–provides a focal point for each of the 26 apartments.

Space, of course, is at a premium in Tokyo, and the majority of apartments in the city are particularly small due to the high cost of land. Conran & Partners are working at the luxury end of the market, making experiments in design that are aimed at building perceptions of value across more traditional building and apartment layouts, both commercially and culturally. Japan's tradition of 'test marketing' – of building and testing prototypes, in advance of full scale production – in industrial design, for instance, provides a convincing precedent here.

The Kamiyamacho apartments' interior layout counter more traditional, compartmentalised Japanese living arrangements with semi-open plan spaces centred on the linking of living room and kitchen. The interiors are simply plastered and painted, with oak floors referencing more traditional Japanese spaces. The building's variety of living areas – the smallest apartment is 70 square metres in size – have been sold to an equal number of Japanese and foreigners. There is a fluidity in the layout of the apartments that sits well between compartmentalised living and completely open loft plans, which can appear bare and lacking in intimacy.

Open plan living, in spite of the 'tatami' mat system of proportion and the habit of rolling up bedding in the daytime, is not commonplace in Japan. At Kamiyamacho one single, generous sized living space acts as the domestic focus, with doors separating it from the more private rooms. Within this simple structure, it is important to find ways of creating visual interest. Hence the apartments are designed in a contemporary style that suits an increasing need for modernity and comfort, without being too avant-garde. Features that make the building individual include the use copper on the curved façade – as only temples in Kyoto and Nara have copper roofs – and the uncommon sight of an entire landscaped roof area.

Both the schemes for Roppongi Hills and Kamiyamacho are clearly Western in their architectural intentions, and represent European housing models brought to the Japanese market. Comparing these developments in Japan with the practice's UK housing is an illuminating exercise, as many of Conran & Partners' UK projects of this type explore the same territory as their Tokyo schemes. Tuthill Stairs, Newcastle; Church Street, Manchester; Drysdale Street, East London; Shirland Mews, London; Tiverton, Devon; and Chandlers, Leeds represent a series of new building projects that each address complex urban issues.

Roppongi Hills in Tokyo constitutes one of the more interesting building sites in Asia, and will soon include Conran & Partners' imprint through the form of a mix of projects, the most conspicuous being two 40 storey apartment towers. A complex masterplan made up of a number of components, each with a different architect, has been developed for the 11 hectare scheme for the Mori Building Company. The other architects involved include Kohn Pedersen Fox (KPF), Fumihiko Maki, and The Jerde Partnership.

The collaboration between Conran & Partners and Mori Building Company originated when a representative from Mori visited the practice's offices at Shad Thames, asking if they knew of someone who could design show flats for them. The subsequent conversation about what was needed led to Minoru Mori, the President of the Mori Building Company, approaching the practice at the end of 1996 to design residential accommodation, as well as retail and office buildings. Conran & Partners' first two completed projects in Tokyo for the client, the Ark Hills Club and the Ark Hills Spa, were well received. The subsequent period of activity has seen the development of two apartment towers and Roppongi Hills Gate, a mixed use scheme that includes shops, offices and housing in ascending order. Other buildings going ahead on the site include an apartment hotel and the Roppongi Hills Club, to be housed on the 51st floor of the KPF building.

The two residential towers are part of the client's overall intention to "meet the needs of many different lifestyles" through the provision of up to 840 new housing units across the four housing blocks. Many buildings in Tokyo are grey and dingy, and in using terracotta tiles and limestone cladding as key materials, the towers offer the generic streetscape an urbane and distinct quality. The terracotta, which provides a rainscreen, is elegant and appears almost as if it were floating. It is part of a palette of materials that are more familiar to a domestic environment than being used for the outside of a building. Unusual in scale and texture, the use of materials here side-steps the more conventional option of a less composite, high tech cladding solution. This concern for a distinct urban language is a hard act to pull off well, but it differentiates the towers from the countless corporate buildings in downtown Tokyo.

Each façade is made up of a series of layers that read through to the inside of each apartment, with inset balconies positioned on a wall of limestone punctuating the front plane of terracotta cladding panels. The balconies are designed as 'micro-landscapes', with planting boxes, timber handrails and decks. Narrower than the full width of the building, the front panel accentuates the building's verticality. Because of the height of the building, getting light into the entire depth of the plan is solved by creating a more spatially ambitious duplex layout, with a double height expression on the façade. On the north façade, the lift cores are articulated as deep vertical grooves and clad in blue glazed tile. The two buildings sit on a three storey podium of car parking and shops, with an entrance pavilion by the practice linking the car parking areas below with the pedestrian plaza. Taking the European references one stage further, landscape architect Dan Pearson has worked with Conran & Partners on a design drawing on the theme of an English copse.

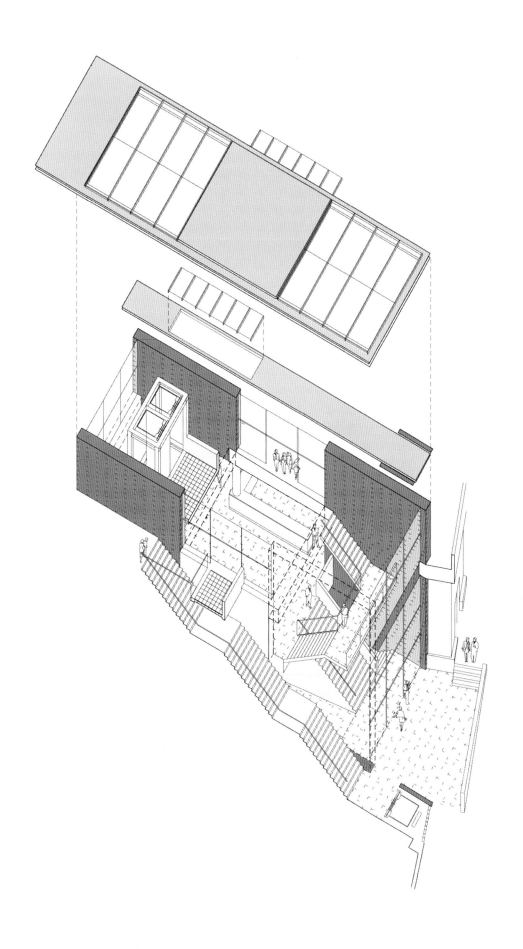

155

Design study of
entrance pavilion
Roppongi Hills

Reception courtyard
Kamiyamacho
Tokyo

Apartment
Living area
Kamiyamacho

UK Housing

Urban design is something Conran & Partners claim has to be based on understanding the ways in which a scheme can be *generative*, and that if thinking about design stays at the level of simple analysis of programme it cannot fulfill this bigger role. Because every site is different, good solutions, they maintain, are about creating an individual, bespoke product – a one-off solution. They see architecture as generating the conditions that allow one to learn further and more fully of what it is to dwell in a city.

A scheme for apartments and commercial premises on the High Street in Manchester, for City Loft Developments, shows how the practice's ideas about urban living are adapted to suit the particular conditions of a city and a site. On the edge of the Smithfield conservation area, the site looks onto the Millennium Masterplan Zone, and aims to acknowledge the plan's strategic objectives by reinforcing the character and atmosphere of this quarter of the city. Adjacent to Conran & Partners' 25 Church Street scheme, the tower has a confident, upbeat presence on the street, and is one of a cluster of tall city centre buildings in the area.

The scheme for the High Street failed to get planning permission owing to a shift in policy, and was subsequently designed as a low-rise building. The original design of the High Street building's five storey sandstone podium, articulated with internal private balconies, relates it to its context aesthetically, with a programme of commercial space that reinforces the existing street level activity. The glass and zinc clad residential tower above reinstates the eroded city block, stepping back to create a commercial entrance on the corner axis, a common feature in the city. It is made up of two interlocking volumes: full height glazed panels and a contrasting zinc-clad service tower wrapping over to create a duplex penthouse. The building shares with its Japanese counterparts the same rich and refined detailing, open lobbies and living spaces.

Visualisation
High Street
Manchester

Church Street
Manchester

Apartment interior
Church Street

Penthouse Interior
Church Street

The loft as a type of domestic living space is a marked symbol of changing lifestyles. Loft developments originated in New York, becoming popular in Central London in the 1990s. With advantage being taken of the huge stock of redundant inner city industrial and commercial building throughout the UK, cities such as Manchester, Birmingham and Liverpool saw a considerable growth in this type of housing. Manchester, in particular, was a pioneer in the loft movement, with developers including Urban Splash and seminal schemes such as the Tobacco Factory based in the city. Conran & Partners, with its track record of breathing new life into redundant historic urban fabric, were co-opted early on as designers of a number of loft ventures. 25 Church Street, the 78 apartment development converted for City Lofts, was a former telecommunications building. Being able to create high quality living space of this kind means knowing how to spend tight budgets in service of a wider urban vision, so that the schemes do not exist purely as isolated 'Shangri-Las', but add an aesthetic generosity alongside the practical and cosmopolitan facilities they contain.

Shirland Mews, a terrace of townhouses in a quiet mews street in London's Maida Vale, is a good example of Conran & Partners' interest in the interaction between contemporary design and historical context. White, crisp and beautifully detailed, it exemplifies the strategy that runs throughout the practice's work of making a transition from old to new, and of bringing change to traditional form and fabric. A more creative approach to residential planning was possible here than in the their more dense urban apartment projects. In a typical London Georgian or Victorian town house, observes Wood, there is often a sectional split between the principal rooms in the main house and ancillary spaces such as former sculleries or smaller bedrooms at the rear of the house. This change in level of three or four steps reduces the size of the staircase and its landing. In a grander town house, access was usually from the rear via a 'mews'. The new town houses at Shirland Mews incorporate and develop elements from these traditional types, with the ground floor maintaining the original mews function, and the split section from the main house being adapted, so as to reduce the stair and its circulation space to the minimum.

Of course, Conran & Partners are no Georgian copyists. The historic structures are accomodated, fully exploiting the changes in level to add drama to the main sequence of living spaces at first floor level. The combined kitchen and dining room are open to and raised half a level above the 'height and a half' living space, resulting in a flowing sequence of spaces throughout each house. The kind of sequencing Conran & Partners adopt is reminiscent of the hall floor piano nobile of a grand Georgian town house, but here the kitchen is included as an important living and communal space. The bedrooms are divided above and below the main living rooms to give a flexibility for guests, lodgers or study space.

The main elevation on the mews is understated. It is a series of full-height openings in a render wall with garage and entrance doors on the ground floor level and a set back terrace on the first floor facing south on to the street. These are both in timber, with a glass and stainless steel balustrade. These features do not add up to a radical intervention, rather they maximise usable floor space with the shift in volume being effectively and tightly controlled. All of this avoids the self-conscious spatial gymnastics of other recent town house developments. Old fabric gets a new lease of life; commercial needs are balanced with the wish to create an innovative contemporary solution.

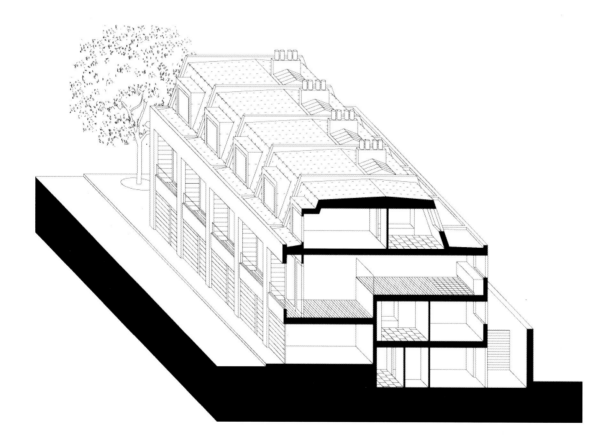

Isometric cross-section
Shirland Mews

Street elevation   Rear elevation   Street view
Shirland Mews

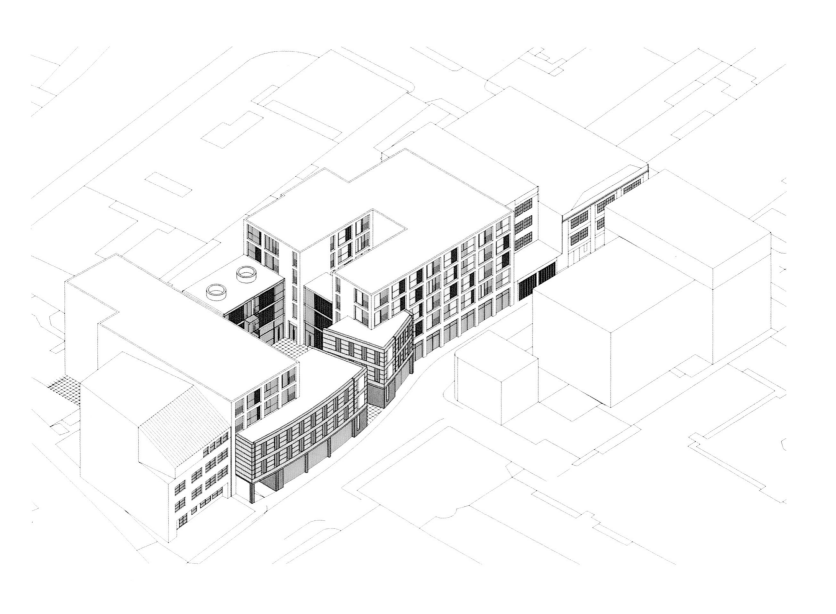

Isometric
Drysdale Street

Street elevation
Drysdale Street

Two projects being developed, Drysdale Street, Hoxton, East London, and Argus House, Brighton, make for an interesting comparison, and show where Conran & Partners stand in terms of current architectural thinking about urban redevelopment and their approach to the rehabilitation of old structures.

The re-use of buildings in Conran & Partners' work raises a number of issues. The "form follows function" axiom of the technocratic branch of the Modern Movement was reversed by Mies van der Rohe in order to make a practical and satisfying shape into which functions could be fitted. Even though financially unsound he justified this as the only practical way to build because the uses to which buildings are put are continually changing. Related to this is the idea that buildings need to be heavy and generic in order to be recycled, in contrast to a high tech approach where buildings become very specific and lightweight. Between these poles Conran & Partners see robust structures with large, regular openings offering the most potential for re-use.

In the Argus House scheme the social housing element of the project is at the foreground in a way that is more continental than English, in the sense of the common juxtaposition of private and social housing given the Dutch cityscape. At the same time, it is a project that responds to different parts of the town, using the opportunity to play off the urban polarities that had developed and do something different. This is the creative territory Conran & Partners describe as "non-design" and "background building".

A lot of the practice's building is about contrast, about accentuating the difference between things, without resorting to pastiche or a deconstructivist vocabulary. Drysdale Street, in particular, typifies this. It is a development that can be read as one of a series of essentially quite modest background buildings which strive to relate to their urban context through a bold architectonic approach, softened by a rich palette of materials. The Drysdale Street intervention takes in the particular detail that makes up this area of London, reflecting Conran & Partners' own observant historical and cultural survey of where they were building.

Just as with the Mori schemes, the overall form and massing at Hoxton were set prior to Conran & Partners' involvement. Existing planning permission for Drysdale Street's former timber yard site set the massing of the scheme. The proposal that got planning approval prior to the architects' involvement was a mock-Edwardian warehouse design, with projecting base elements in concrete and contrasting brickwork. In the practice's redesign of the building the two main blocks became rigorous brick grids containing assemblies of glazing, balustrades and sliding screens. This follows the explorations seen in the Mori work as well as closer to home at the Tuthill Stairs development in Newcastle.

The street frontage makes a bold statement, with its gently curving zinc belly highly visible from Hoxton Street. The main massing, with it's ordered grid, can be discerned in earlier Conran Roche studies, but with a richness and layering that became prevalent in the practice's work throughout the 1990s. Steel and glass 'insertions' are devices repeatedly used at Butler's Wharf, as well as in more recent projects such as Crescent Buildings, Harrogate. The practice first included grass roofs as an architectural feature in the Longman project, a rare sight in 1995. Now it is much more common and the grass roofs on the projecting lower buildings at Hoxton exploit the desire for green space in this gritty part of the city.

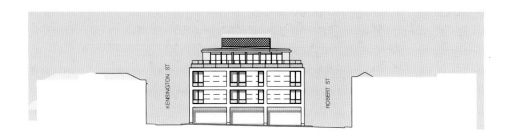
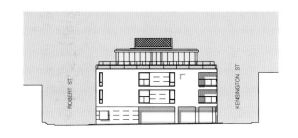

Street elevations
Argus House

The Argus scheme, while taking its cue from Brighton's surrounding streets and the impact on these of years of blighted 1960s and 70s urban 'regeneration', is a project that required the sensitive conversion of old buildings and the design and construction of new ones. Here, clearly, was the opportunity to explore many key interests held by the practice – a mixed use scheme incorporating apartments, shops, restaurants, workshops, and a venue for the Brighton Fringe Festival. There was, as well, a planning requirement for social housing on the site, which gave Conran & Partners the opportunity to explore ideas developed in housing projects with higher budgets in a scheme governed by significant cost constraints.

The urban block that makes up the site is a rare exception in the area, in that it never contained housing, but was, for most of the twentieth century, the home of *The Evening Argus*, Brighton's local newspaper. The site is in four parts – at the southern end, a poor quality 1960s office building sits incongruously on a mid-to late Victorian street. To the north, an ornate, early twentieth century brick building by Samuel Denman sits next to a slightly later industrial building, with the site ending in a small vacant plot at its northern end. The context for the architecture came from the rendered houses of the surrounding area, the industrial building on the site and, above all, the particular, quirky character of the neighbourhood. At the southern end, the 60s office is being re-clad and extended to create a framed, rendered building for social housing provision. The exploration of frame and infill is a common theme in Conran & Partners' work, and here the adoptions are an optimistic, forward looking response to the locality and its conservation area, as well as Rab Bennetts' new Brighton Library scheme due to be built across the road. The render of the surrounding streets is contrasted by the diverse range of coloured panels inspired by the underlying general playfulness of the area. The roofs are edged with zinc planters and the setback top floors screened with bamboo – an attempt to use these roof areas to green this dense urban environment.

The new building at the northern end has more solid elevations, responding directly to the conservation area. A stone base is punctured by display windows for shops, with tight windows above the rendered walls where they directly face nearby buildings, as well as larger openings to catch afternoon sun. There is a memory of the framed composition here, but tempered by the immediate conditions and more directly linked to the practice's work on the Design Museum than the rigorous grids of Milton Keynes.

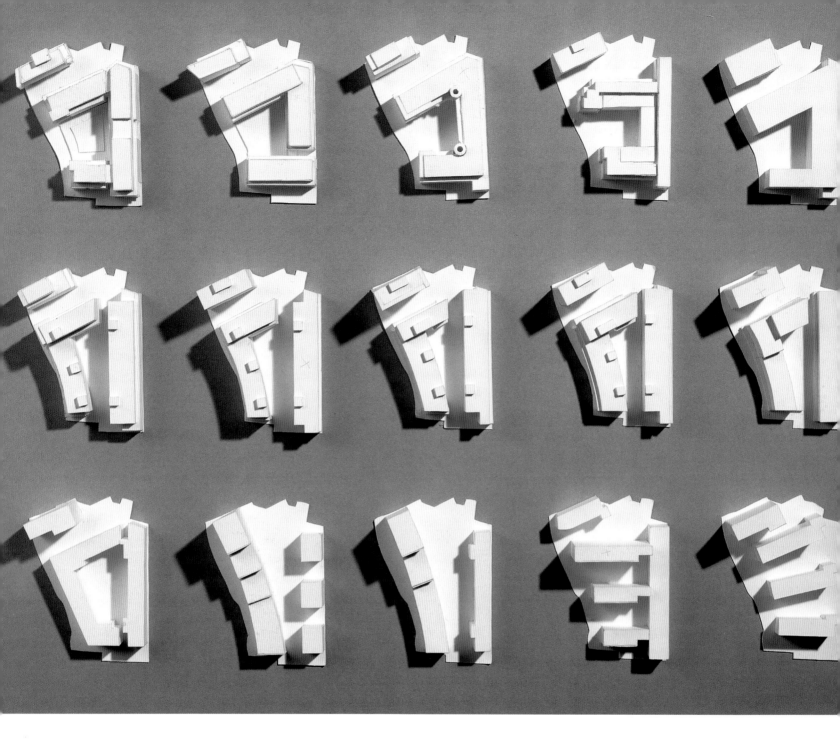

Option study models
The Chandlers

The issue of context is always an individual matter. The Chandlers, two new buildings adjacent to the River Aire in Leeds, and a relatively large new development of 90 apartments, addresses the question of what kind of contemporary design is valid in an important conservation area. Another Northern city largely destroyed by crass Post War development, Leeds has seen new focus paid to the regeneration of its urban fabric. By contrast, the more rurally sited housing designed at Tiverton, Devon, is interesting because it promotes repetition as an asset rather than something to avoid. A solution for speculative estate development, it uses formal layouts and landscaping. Indeed, there is a generosity in its spatial planning, which can be seen in terms of a re-visiting of the idea of 1960s open planning.

Conran & Partners' solution for Tuthill Stairs, a complex site in the centre of Newcastle, has been referred to by English Heritage as "an almost classical design without any contextual references", "coolly independent", and with a "relentless adherence to geometry". However, on closer analysis, the scheme seems rather more integrated than these remarks might imply. A development of 72 apartments and 830 square metres of ground floor restaurant space, it occupies a prominent location overlooking the river Tyne. It is a brownfield site, unfortunately renowned for drugs and prostitution, in the west Quayside area of the city centre – the type of urban location the government's Urban Task Force report identified as a high priority for redevelopment. Designed in accordance with the City Council's vision for the regeneration of the area, which includes extending Quayside activity westwards toward Forth Banks, it offers a significant future residential development for the city.

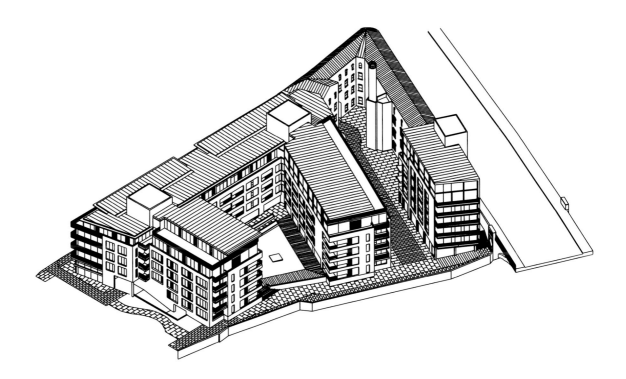

Isometric
The Chandlers

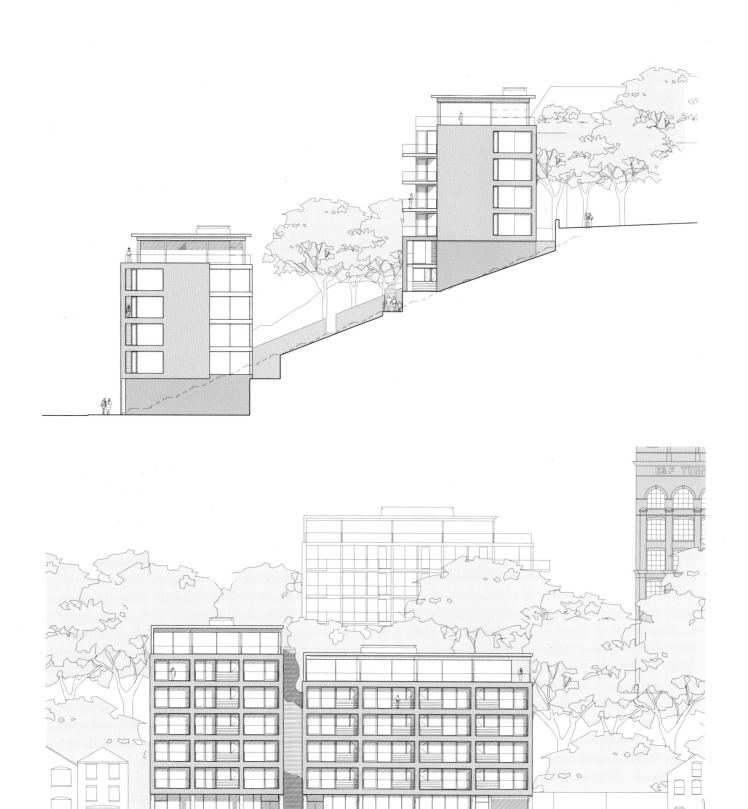

Elevations
Tuthill Stairs

Newcastle has recently seen the completion of Chris Wilkinson's 'winking eye' bridge, with Norman Foster's Music Centre currently under construction, and Dominic Williams' Baltic Centre in Gateshead due to open in 2002. This cultural shift in the city is complemented by new high quality apartment buildings and these public facilities complement their ambition. The site, which was once the centre of town, has long been cut off from the current centre by a high level bridge. The three new buildings planned will straddle the ancient route of Tuthill Stairs. The first two flank the stairs at the bottom of the hill, and are sheltered from the busy road. To reach the third, at the top of the hill, the stair route is realigned to form a 'funnel'. The overall massing of the buildings forms a spiral, stepping up the slope of the hillside, where an old warehouse building maintains its dominance.

Both in setting and composition the trio of buildings is indicative of Conran & Partners' ability to create an attractive and practical environment. The scheme accords with the vision of 'clustering' that the architects Llewelyn-Davies proposed to the City Council in a study of development options for the area around Newcastle Central Station. The first building has been designed to signal the threshold into this zone, with the elevations of all three buildings sharing an architectural language that uses materials including a brick grid and layers of timber, glazing, render and metal panels. On the east and west elevations a steel grid faces the landscaped areas on either side. This is open public space that the practice want to re-unite through the positioning of the project. A 'landswap' offered by the council to reposition one of the buildings within this area, in return for green space at the heart of the scheme allows this rationalisation to occur without loss of public open space. In a further attempt to provide a solution that is in context, these elevations read at the same height as the Victorian buildings throughout the city. The setback of the top level of the buildings from the north and south elevations reduces its impact and provides terraces for the penthouses contained within. This level is designed as an inverted 'L' and clad in zinc, emphasising views of the city and the Tyne bridge to the east.

Prospective projects such as Tuthill Stairs, for an industrial city in the process of throwing off the redundant elements of its past, are indicative of an architectural sensibility that endeavours to decipher the social condition of a situation and forge schemes using an architectural language that forms a mediatory role within an environment. In the process of such interventions, the past can be made to speak more powerfully, with history, as Conran & Partners' own work demonstrates, being allowed the possibility to be understood in new ways. The practice, in welcoming and responding to change on all levels, is marked by an *inclusive* mentality and *generalist* ability to play a unique role within culture. And their work, as described in this book, distinctly presents a generosity and divergence of strategies that offer a highly perceptive vision of the public realm.

following pages   Main entrance   Façade Detail   Car Park   Mall   Rotunda   Food Terrace
Ocean Terminal
Edinburgh

Architecture and Interiors
(dates are completion dates for built projects, design dates for unbuilt projects – awards and key publications listed)

1983
Butlers Wharf Masterplan
4.5 ha docklands site in the Tower Bridge conservation area, 1983-1995. Built projects include museums, restaurants, infrastructure works, residential accommodation, galleries, retail and office space – listed individually. Unbuilt projects include Butlers Court – mixed use live/work, retail, commercial, 1988, W-Court – residential/cinema, 1988, and Butler's (Grinders and Operators) Site – primarily residential, 1988, includes re-located Wheat Wharf building, 1997. Further masterplanning took place in 1993 (see later entry)
> Architecture Today May 1989
> Architect's Journal 16 May 1990

1984
Institute of Chartered Accountants Headquarters
Silbury Boulevard,
Central Milton Keynes
3,800 sq m headquarters building for the Institute of Chartered Accountants of England and Wales
> Architect's Journal 7 Aug 1985

Pericom
Rockingham Drive, Linford Wood, Milton Keynes
3,000 sq m industrial unit for Pericom plc

1985
Heathrow Causeway
152-176 Great South West Road, Hounslow
8 industrial units for Conran Roche Limited

1986
County Court
Silbury Boulevard,
Central Milton Keynes
1600 sq m building including court room, judge's and advocates' suites and a public area for Property Services Agency

Habitat
Fitzwilliam Street, Cambridge
Refurbishment of store and new retail units for Habitat Ltd

Mothercare Distribution Centre
Wellingborough
25,000 sq m National Distribution Centre providing storage volume of 310,000 m³ for Mothercare UK

Post House Hotel
Saxon Gate,
Central Milton Keynes
164 bed 11,500 sq m hotel with health club forming part of the Central Business Exchange for Trusthouse Forte Hotels

1987
Cinnamon Wharf
Shad Thames, London SE1
Conversion of 1950s apartment building to 66 flats overlooking St Saviour's Dock and Shad Thames. Including studios, one and two bed apartments and penthouses for Butler's Wharf Limited

Michelin House
Brompton Road, London
Restoration and conversion of the Grade II listed Michelin Building to 11,150 sq m of retail, Bibendum Restaurant and Oyster Bar and office space for Terence Conran, Paul Hamlyn and the English Tourist Board
> Award RIBA
    London Regional Award
> Europa Nostra Award
> Civic Trust Commendation
> BBC Design Award 1990 runner-up
> Architect's Journal Mar 1988
> Building Design Mar 1988
> RIBA Journal Mar 1988
> Architectural Review (USA)
    Oct 1988

1988
Bravo
Aberdeen
Oil Experience Centre – study centre for the North Sea oil industry for Aberdeen Beyond 2000 (unbuilt)

Greenland Dock,
Lock Control Building and Pier
Greenland Dock
Surrey Quays, London SE16
3.25 ha masterplan, infrastructure works, pier and lock control building for London Docklands Development Corporation
> RTPI Award for Planning
    Achievement 1989
> RICS Inner Cities Award 1988
> Architect's Journal 14 Nov 1990
> Building 11 May 1990

1989
Blueprint Café
Shad Thames, London SE1
96 cover restaurant in the Design Museum for Conran Restaurants Limited

Butlers Wharf Building
Shad Thames, London SE1
Conversion of Grade II listed Thames-side warehouse to 98 apartments. restaurants, shops and offices for Butlers Wharf Limited
> Civic Trust Commendation 1991

Coriander Building
Gainsford Street, London SE1
1,430 sq m conversion of warehouse to office for Butler's Wharf Limited

Design Museum
Shad Thames, London SE1
3,700 sq m conversion of derelict warehouse to world's first museum of design for The Conran Foundation
> RIBA Architecture Award
> Eternit International Prize
> English Tourist Board Award
> Europa Nostra
> BBC Design Award 1990 runner-up
> EC Design Prize
> Civic Trust Commendation 1991
> Architect's Journal 16 Aug 1989
> Blueprint 24 July 1989
> Bauwelt Dec 1990
> RIBA Journal Aug 1989

LSE Student Residence
Gainsford Street, London SE1
280 bed student residence building for London School of Economics

Nutmeg House
Gainsford Street, London SE1
2,000 sq m conversion to office and nursery for Butler's Wharf Limited

1990

Butler's Wharf Infrastructure
Butler's Wharf, London SE1
York stone and granite quayside and
street paving, new lighting, seating and
pier structure for Butler's Wharf Limited

Campbell Park Business Village
Campbell Park, Central Milton Keynes
Office pavilions, serviced office building,
studios for living and working and
residential units for Campbell Park
Developments Limited (unbuilt)

Cardamon Building
Shad Thames, London SE1
Refurbishment and conversion of five
Grade II listed warehouse buildings to
64 residential units linked by bridges
to the Butler's Wharf Building for
Butler's Wharf Limited

Saffron Wharf
Shad Thames, London SE1
2,250 sq m of new build air-conditioned
office facing St Saviour's Dock and
Shad Thames for Butler's Wharf Limited
> Architect's Journal 16 May 1990

New Crane Wharf
Wapping Wall, London E1
New build and refurbished warehouse
creating 143 apartments for Conran
Roche Developments/Heron Homes
> Mansell Refurbishment Design
  Award Commendation 1990
> Building Design Aug 1990
> House & Garden Jul 1990

1991

Howland Quay
Surrey Quays, London SE18
Two 'green' office buildings (unbuilt)
for London Dockland Development
Corporation
> Building Design May 1992

1992

Hays Distribution Centre
Brinklow, Milton Keynes
2,800 sq m distribution warehouse
and offices for Hays Distribution
Services Limited

Landmark Place
Central Milton Keynes
Two office buildings, totalling 8,000
sq m around the new City Church
for Beazer Developments

1993

Butlers Wharf Re-masterplanning
1993-1995, including: Building 15,
2 schemes (tower and lower building)
Butler's – Grinders and Operators – site,
conversion and new residential buildings
Spice Hotel and Spice Quay Residential
Buildingfor Ernst & Young (all unbuilt)

1994

Buckingham Palace
London SW1
Temporary visitor facilities for the
first opening of Buckingham Palace
to the general public for Royal
Collection Enterprises

Conran Shop
Shinsuku Park Tower, Tokyo
1,300 sq m store for Tokyo Gas

Metropolitan Hotel
Old Park Lane, London W1
Concept work for hotel refurbishment
for Comojo (UK) Limited

Clarence Hotel
Room concept design work for the
Dublin hotel for two members of U2

1995

Addison Wesley
Longman Headquarters
Harlow, Essex
New-build 15,300 sq m headquarters
for Addison Wesley Longman
> Architect's Journal 30 May 1996

Black Eagle Wharf
Wapping High Street, London E1
Planning approval for new Thames-side
apartment building – 84 flats,
implemented by others, now Capital
Wharf – for Fairclough Homes

Butler's Wharf Chef School
Shad Thames, London SE1
Chef training school and restaurant
for Butler's Wharf Chef School

Café Lux
The Academy, Aberdeen (unbuilt)
Concept work for new café for Jarlaw

Clarkes' Mews
Marylebone, London W1
Mews house refurbishment
for Mr and Mrs Heyderman

Clove Building
Maguire Street, London SE1
Fit-out of 840 sq m of office space
for Conran Restaurants

Das Triest
Wiedner Hauptstrasse, Vienna
73 bed hotel, including
restaurant, bar and common parts
for Hoffman Maculan

Dunlop Semtex Factory
Brynmawr, Wales
Proposals for the conversion of
the Brynmawr Rubber Factory to
leisure use for South Wales Leisure
Developments (not implemented)

Globe Wharf
Rotherhithe, London
Feasibility Study for conversion of
riverside warehouse to apartments
for Fairclough Homes

Hammersmith Hotel
London W8
Design of day room for Teenage
Cancer Trust

Haymarket
Hammersmith, London W8
Exterior treatment, reception area and
executive suite for Haymarket Publishing

Emporium
Hartlepool
Designer clothing factory outlet within
Jacksons Landing building, in the newly
regenetrated docks for Sovereign Land

King and Queen Wharf
Rotherhithe Conversion of retail units
to apartment, for Fairclough Homes

Le Petit Blanc
Walton Street, Oxford
125 cover restaurant in Oxford including
a bar, main restaurant and salon prive
for Raymond Blanc

Mezzo
Wardour Street, London W1
700 cover restaurants, bars and shops
for Conran Restaurants
> 1996 Design Week Award
> Architect's Journal 28 Sept 1995

No 1 Aldwych
London W1
Planning approval for conversion of
listed building to 120 bed hotel for
Hemisphere Hotels

Premier
Selfridges, Oxford Street, London W1
100 cover restaurant on the 5th floor
of Selfridges department store for
Selfridges plc

Sussan
Melbourne, Australia
New womensware retail concept
for Sussan

Zinc Bar and Grill
Heddon Street, London W1
New bar concept for Conran
Restaurants

1996

Conran Shop
Fukuoka, Japan
New store in Japan for Tokyo Gas

Conran Shop
Stillwerk, Gr. Elbstrasse, Hamburg
1,700 sq m shop for The Conran Shop

Loizias
Design concept work for restaurant
in Smithfield for Louis Loizia
(not implemented)

Royaly House
Soho, London
Office planning and fit out for
Conran Restaurants

Ridley Scott Offices
London
Refurbishment schemes for Beak
Street Headquarters of production
company for RSA (not implemented)

Vespa Café
Concept work for new cafés and retail
outlets for Vespa (not implemented)

1997

Bluebird
King's Road, Chelsea, London SW3
Conversion of Grade II Listed
garage, to food market, restaurant
and club for Bluebird Store
Limited/Harris & Webber
> Architectural Review July 1997
> Architect's Journal 12 June 1997
> Civic Trust Award 1998

Blueprint Café Extension
Shad Thames, London SE1
New glass structure to extend dining
area for Conran Restaurants

Conran Shop
Marylebone High Street, London, W1
3400 sq m new building incorporating
retained section of old stables building
for The Conran Shop and Orrery
Restaurant for Conran Restaurants
> Civic Trust Commendation 1999
> Architects Journal 5th March 1998
> 50 Trade Secrets of Great Design
> Retail Spaces, Stafford Cliff

DDB Needham
Paris
Design Concept competition for
advertising agency for DDB Needham
(not implemented)

Godman
London
Production company offices for
Godman Limited
> The Creative Office by
  Jeremy Myerson

Lenbach
Munich
Restaurant and bar designed around
the theme of the Seven Deadly Sins
for Michael Kafer

Marlborough Place
Maida Vale, London
Refurbishment of house
for private client

Pavone Café
Princes Square, Glasgow
Graphics, layout and furniture
improvements for Pavone Cafe

Quaglinos
London
Re-working of bar area in restaurant
for Conran Restaurants

Stanley Street Store
Scheme for conversion of Liverpool's
former head post office to major new
retail development (not implemented)
for The Walton Group

1998

Air, Ark + Alu
Dusseldorf, Germany
Three cafe/bars in Dusseldorf Airport
for Stockheim

Alcazar
Paris
Restaurant, bar and brasserie
for Conran Restaurants

Britannia Visitors Centre
Leith, Edinburgh
Temporary visitors centre for
Royal Yacht Britannia for Forth Ports

Cafetiero
Coffee shop 'roll-out' design
for Stockheim

Conran Collection
Conduit Street, London
Home to the Conran Collection range
of products for The Conran Shop
Coq D'Argent, London
Restaurant and bar on the roof of
No 1 Poultry for Conran Restaurants

Design Museum Extension
Winning entry for works to expand
and improve the Museum for The
Design Museum (not implemented)

Fitzwilliam Hotel
St Stephen's Green, Dublin
110 room contemporary hotel for
The Fitzwilliam Hotel Group

Georges
Central Melbourne
Department Store refurbishment,
including restaurants and cafes
for Georges Limited

Hamilton Palace Grounds Retail Park
Competition for new retail park in
Hamilton, Scotland for Miller
Developments (not implemented)

Maison et Objet
Paris homewares exhibition
for Maison et Objet

Metropolitan, Glasgow
50,000 sq m cinema and leisure
complex for MEPC/Miller
(not implemented)

Rex Bar
Reykjavik
Bar and restaurant for Isfossar

Sartoria
Savile Row, London
Restaurant and bar for
Conran Restaurants

Spirit & Sienna
Trafford Centre, Manchester
Restaurants in new Selfridges
store for Selfridges plc

1999

**"From the Bomb to
the Beatles 1945-65"**
Exhibition for Imperial War Museum

Ark Hills Club
Tokyo
Private dining club (incorporating
display spaces for client's collection
of Le Corbusier paintings) for
Mori Corporation

Berns Restaurants
Central Stockholm
Restaurants, bars and café in
historic building for Berns Hotel/
Conran Restaurants

Bute Gardens
Hammersmith, London
External works and new reception
for Haymarket Publishing

Chelsea Flower Show
The Chef's Roof Garden
for the Evening Standard
> Gold Medal Winner

Concorde Room
JFK Airport, New York
Airport lounge for Concorde
travellers for British Airways

Conran Shop
Berlin
New store for The Conran Shop

Conran Shop
Capucines, Paris
Second Paris store for
The Conran Shop

Heathcoat House
Saville Row, London
Reception area for London and
Devonshire Trust

**Leith, Granton and Newhaven
Masterplans**
Illustrative plans for Edinburgh's
Waterfront for Forth Ports plc

Mezzo Café
Wardour Street, London
Re-working of cafe in Mezzo
for Conran Restaurants

St Johns Square
London
Sketch designs for office building
with restaurant on ground floor for
Mr Mahboubian (not implemented)

London Business School
Reception area re-design for
Dean of School (not implemented)

Queen Margaret College
Studies for new campus on sites
on Edinburgh's Waterfront for
Forth Ports plc (not implemented)

2000

25 Church Street, Manchester
10,176 sq m residential conversion
of former cotton warehouse
for City Loft Developments Limited

Ark Hills Spa & Health Club
Tokyo
New Spa for Mori Building Company

Bloomberg
Competition for office designs
for agency for Bloomberg
(not implemented)

Bridgemarket
New York
Restaurants, bar and premises
for The Conran Shop beneath
the arches of the Queensboro Bridge,
Manhattan, includes new entrance
pavilion building for Conran Holdings

Coffee Kiosk
Coffee Shop Concept
for Conran Restaurants

Concept House
Competition entry for Ideal Home
Exhibition (not implemented)

Conran Shop
Dusseldorf, Germany
New store for The Conran Shop

Great Eastern Hotel
Liverpool Street, London EC2
Redevelopment of the City of London's
only hotel, includes the restaurants
Aurora, Fishmarket, Georges and
Terminus, and Train gym for Conran
Holdings/Wyndham International

Grosvenor Buildings, Harrogate
Residential development
for City Lofts Limited
> Civic Trust Commendation 2000

Kamiyamacho
Tokyo
Five storey residential development
for Mori Building Company

"London Eats Out" Exhibition
Five centuries of eating out in London
for Museum of London

Museum of London Galleries
Two new galleries as part of current
refurbishment of museum for
Museum of London

Myhotel
London
73 bedroom contemporary town
house hotel for Myhotels

Royal Infirmary
Edinburgh
Shortlisted competition entry, mixed
use scheme for re-use of hospital site,
conversion of listed buildings and
addition of new buildings for Wilson
Bowden (not implemented)

Southwark Site
London
Studies for 40,000 sq m mixed use
scheme north of Elephant & Castle for
Hollybrook (not implemented)

Tiverton
Residential development for London
and Devonshire Trust Limited
(not implemented)

Vialli Apartment
Eaton Place, London
Refurbishment of flat for Gianluca Vialli

Vision Express
New design concept for UK retail
outlets for Grand Vision

Zinc Bar and Grill
Manchester
Bar and grill in the Triangle (formerly
the Corn Exchange) for Conran
Restaurants

2001

Ark Hills Spa
Tokyo
Delicatessen and cafe/restuarant
associated with Ark Hills Spa for Mori
Building Company

Ark Towers
Tokyo
Apartment design in residential
development for Mori Building Company

Concorde House
Heathrow, Terminal 4, London
New lounge for 1st Class and
Concorde passengers for
British Airways

Forest Hill Gate Tower
Tokyo
Mixed use development –
residential, retail and office for
Mori Building Company

Glassworks Gym
850 sq m gymnasium opposite
Magdalen College for Cambridge
Renaissance
> Vogue June 2001

Labour Party
Works to Millbank Headquarters,
including meeting rooms and
reception for The Labour Party

Motoazabu
Tokyo
Three apartment designs for
Mori Building Company

Myhotel 5th Floor
London
New penthouse suites above
existing hotel for Myhotel

Ocean Terminal
Leith, Edinburgh
60,000 sq m shopping and leisure
building for Forth Properties Limited

**Ocean Terminal Food Terrace
and Zinc Bar**
Fit out of food terrace and restaurant
unit within Ocean Terminal Shopping
Centre for Conran Restaurants

Park Hotel
Bangalore, India
Refurbishmeht of 100 bedroom
hotel for Park Hotels

RIBA Bar
London
Refurbishment of Florence Hall
restaurant/exhibition space for
Royal Institute of British Architects

Uniqlo
New store designs for Japanese
clothing retailer for Uniqlo

Wolverton Gardens
Hammersmith, London
New office building for
Haymarket Publishing

Zinc Bar and Grill
Central Birmingham
Zinc Bar and Grill on canal-side
for Conran Restaurants

Current

38 High Street Manchester
New apartment building 5,150 sq m
for City Loft Developments

Alcazar Club
Paris
Nightclub in vaults below existing
restaurant for Conran Restaurants

Argus House
Brighton
New and refurbished buildings,
apartments and commercial space
for City Loft Developments

B + C Entrance Pavilion
Roppongi, 6-Chome, Tokyo
Steel and glass concierge and
reception building for two taller
towers for Mori Building Company

Casina Valadier
Central Rome
Studies for new restaurants
and bars for Conran Restaurants

C Block
Roppongi, 6-Chome, Tokyo
Design of two 42 storey residential
towers and one 18 storey tower as
part of major mixed use development
for Mori Building Company

Chandlers
Leeds
New housing scheme on
River Aire for Linfoot plc

Churchill China
Studies for masterplanning site of
factory in Stoke and provision of new
visitor centre for Churchill China

C Tower Apartments,
Roppongi, 6-Chome, Tokyo
Three apartment designs for
Mori Building Company

C Block Landscape
Roppongi, 6-Chome, Tokyo
Landscaping of roof to podium at
base of towers, with Dan Pearson,
for Mori Building Company

Drysdale Street
Hoxton, London
New build apartments, live/work and
commercial space for City Lofts

D Tower Serviced Apartments
Roppongi, 6-Chome, Tokyo
Three serviced apartment designs
for Mori Building Company

Guilford Civic
Designs for two sites in Central
Guildford, including new civic theatre,
hotels, offices, retail and apartments
for Richardson Developments

Harewood Quarter
New retail and residential
scheme in Central Leeds for
Town Centre Securities

Lawrence Graham
Studies for reception area for
legal firm in Central London for
Lawrence Graham

Merchant Village
70,000 sq m mixed use
redevelopment of Glasgow's
Merchant City for Pathfinder plc

Myhotel
Central Glasgow
Conversion of historic building in
the city to second Myhotel
for Myhotel

Niki Club
Nasu, Japan
New hotel for Niki Club Hotels

Parkfield Street
Islington, London
Architectural advisors to funders
of retail and leisure development
for Delancey Estates

Plymouth
Studies for locating new residential
tower, offices and conference
facilities on a site above Sutton
Harbour for Belvedere

Queen's Wharf
Queen's Road, Reading
Architectural advice, layout planning
and interior design of apartment,
conversion from office building for
City Loft Developments

Roppongi Hills Club
Roppongi, 6-Chome, Tokyo
Private members club on the 51st
floor of new tower development for
Mori Building Company

St Anne's Quay
Newcastle upon Tyne
Interior designs for new apartment
building on Newcastle's Quayside
for City Lofts

Shirland Mews
London
Town houses and mews houses
in Shirland Mews, Maida Vale
for Q Developments Limited

Tuthill Stairs
Newcastle upon Tyne
3 new apartment buildings in
Central Newcastle for City Lofts